BIG
BUSINESS
LEADERS
IN
AMERICA

BIG BUSINESS LEADERS IN AMERICA

BY

W. Lloyd Warner

Professor of Sociology, University of Chicago

AND

James C. Abegglen

Instructor, Committee on Human Development,
University of Chicago

Harper & Brothers : New York

To the memory of Elton Mayo

Contents

List of Charts

BIG
BUSINESS
LEADERS
IN
AMERICA

1

The Careers of American
Business Leaders

What the Book Is About

The great industrial and business empires that extend across America and penetrate most of the public and private activities of our daily lives are of deep concern to all of us and vitally important to the well-being of our country. At the top of each of these great business hierarchies is a small group of powerful leaders who order and control its vast operations. Together they constitute the leadership of big business in America. Chairmen of the board, presidents, vice presidents, and others who compose top management, they direct our industrial armies. Although numbered in the tens of thousands, their proportion to the total number of men and women employed in business and industry is small. They occupy those powerful positions where policies and ultimate decisions are made which result in concerted actions throughout their organizations—actions which affect all of us. Above their level in their organizations frequently there is no one; below are thousands who accept their orders and do their bidding.

Whether we approve or disapprove, much of what we now are and hope to be as a nation and a people is founded on the solid economic base of Big Business and on the moral judgments and intellectual capacities of its leaders. Iron, coal, and steel, furniture and food, automobiles and telephones, as well as radio, television, motion pictures, and many other commodities and services, in part are controlled and organized by these vast industrial enterprises. Many of these organizations, including some in banking and

1

finance, reach beyond our national boundaries and spread throughout the free world. Now that America's influence on the political and economic life of the world is often crucial and always powerful and significant, the policies, decisions, and activities of these great corporations and the men who run them help determine whether our kind of civilization and our political and economic order will survive.

The careers of the "business tycoons," their private lives, and what they are thought to be have become the material of legend, folk song, and the modern theater. Some of them have been transformed by the popular mind into symbols and stereotypes on which Americans project their hostilities and frustrations, as well as their hopes, wishes, and aspirations for their own tomorrows. Contemporary novels sometimes describe what these men are believed to be as persons and interpret the social and moral significance of their careers. Theodore Dreiser's *The Titan*, Frank Norris' *The Octopus*, *The Big Money* by John Dos Passos, *Point of No Return* by John Marquand, and many others attempt this task, some of them objectively, most with hostility, a few with favorable intent. All recognize the significance of such men for Americans and the dramatic impact of their lives on the American mentality. Because our feelings and thoughts about them are filled with conflicting emotions, the public understanding of what big business men are and what they do to become what they are, of how they rise to power and position, and why they are successful, is often confused. Public discussion about them blazes with controversy: for some they are heroes who lead the armies of progress; for others they are evil destroyers or "robber barons" who plunder the public of its common wealth.

Although we need art to provide insight into the persons and meaning of the business elite, we also must arm ourselves with the knowledge of science to help us make sound judgments about them. The present volume presents a scientific study of these men. It tells what kind of men they are, how they climbed to the top levels of American enterprise, why they succeeded, and their mean-

ing and significance for Americans. It presents the results of studying the life careers of over eight thousand business leaders from all
industries and from every state. It is a study of their social and
occupational origins and continuing careers and their rise to wealth
and power; it is also a report on the psychological foundations of
their personalities. It not only analyzes their business careers and
the occupations of their fathers and grandfathers but also exam-
ines the economic backgrounds of their wives and their wives'
fathers.

The social and economic facts of the occupational career of the
man and his family do not tell the whole story. Therefore, the private worlds of some of the men were also explored by depth interviewing. This procedure was followed by careful psychological examination of their personalities to learn what within them drove
or led them to success. From these studies we believe we have
answers to some of the questions and concerns about these men.

Many Americans believe that the American Dream of climbing
from the bottom to positions of great power can no longer be
fulfilled. They are convinced that the seats of the mighty are
now permanently reserved for the sons and families of the business
elite. They assert that aspiring men of today born to low position,
who possess the necessary pluck, will-to-do, and ability to accumulate, can no longer work their way into the top positions of Big
Business. Yesterday American society, many believe, was fluid and
open; it invited men of strong will and brains to pour their energies
into the economic life of the nation and encouraged their advancement by rewarding them with prestige, power, wealth, and position.
But today, grown more rigid, it is alleged, our country has closed
the doors to advancement and mobility up from the lower ranks of
life to high position. Is America no longer a land of opportunity?
Are we becoming a "caste-like" society? Are we less democratic
than in past generations, and is equality of opportunity reduced
or no longer available for those with the talent, skill, and will-to-do?

We ask and answer the question: Is it possible today for men
coming from families at the lowest occupational levels, the un-

skilled industrial and farm laborers, or those from the skilled trades and the white-collar classes to reach the top as they did in the past? And if so, do they succeed today as much as, or more than, a generation ago? Is opportunity in America greater today, or is the American Dream legend and fantasy and no longer within the realm of fact and reality? Taussig and Joslyn, of the Economics Department of Harvard University, predicted that by the middle of this century occupational advancement from lower levels into the business elite would have largely disappeared. Following their significant study of American business leaders of 1928, they declared: "It is entirely possible that by the middle of the century more than two-thirds of the successful businessmen in the United States will be recruited from the sons of business owners (large or small) and business executives (major or minor)."[1]

The ambivalent values present in all Americans about the inter-relations of individual achievement and romantic love are clearly stated by the ethical conflict in their minds about "marrying the boss's daughter" or other women of superior social levels. American magazines and popular novels dramatize the problems of the woman who marries beneath herself, they tell about the man ("bad") who marries the wealthy woman and rejects the girl he loved, or more often the poor boy ("good") who marries the boss's daughter and then by hard work and ability proves himself by climbing into a position in the firm equal to the one he married ("very good").

Today it is sometimes cynically said that it is better to train sons to learn how to attract a wealthy wife than to train them for advancement; or better to introduce them to the right people, on the principle that it is "who you know not what you know" that gets you ahead. We attempted to find the answers to such questions when we asked: What were the economic levels of the women when they married their husbands? If the business leader comes from the wrong side of the tracks does he advance his

[1] F. W. Taussig and C. S. Joslyn, *American Business Leaders* (New York: The Macmillan Company, 1932), p. 235.

career by marrying above himself or does he marry someone at his own level and, out of this marital partnership where each helps the other, achieve the prestigeful place he now occupies? How many men of the business elite marry the boss's daughter? How many marry the girl around the corner?

To increase our knowledge of the problem of status and marriage we turned the question around and asked: What kind of men do *ambitious women* marry? How many of the *women* born to lowly status marry well above themselves into the business elite?

Since the life careers of ambitious women usually are not in professional roles but are realized by marriage to "a successful catch," sometimes aided by the skilled manipulations of a clever mother, one must ask what kind of human beings these women are? Do they marry for love? Are the marriages of men born to high status, the birth elite, successful? Are they more likely to marry women of their own high status or is the Cinderella story in fact a frequent one? And, if it is, are such Cinderellas women who love their mates and make successful marriages or are they egocentric destroyers who value social and economic advancement as of ultimate importance and marriage as no more than a legal mechanism to achieve their selfish goals?

"The Wives of Ambitious Men" and "The Kinds of Women Who Make Successful Wives" (Chapters VI and VII) tell the story of the economic and social backgrounds of the wives, the roles they play in the careers of the business leaders, and the private worlds and personality structures of these women of the business elite.

The whole family, as well as the wife, is deeply involved in the upward advancement of the son, father, or husband. Some men turn their business success into a full life and into social and personal success. Some families make good social adjustments, some do not; some men make good fathers and husbands, some are failures. Some wives are social failures while their husbands are economically successful. Some men and their wives, outwardly successful, live mentally on dead-end streets where, isolated and lonely, they serve time waiting for their careers to end. Several chapters present evidence on how much and in what ways families and relatives, particularly fathers, helped or hindered the career of the business leader.

Most parents today who wish their sons to achieve or who, like most Americans, simply want their children to have "more of a chance than I had" think in terms of a good education. Sometimes this means college and even postgraduate degrees; sometimes it means no more than graduation from high school. It is often alleged that no one can get ahead today without a college degree, that the youngster fresh out of grade school, starting at the bottom, assigns himself to a lifetime of menial labor. Is this true? Such an opinion is often enforced in the public mind by the knowledge that today most big businesses have recruiting programs which bring carefully selected college graduates into their firms for training, thus favoring their advancement over the "uneducated Horatio Algers."

Higher education, now considered the "royal road to promotion and pay," has always been used in America by the upper levels. Since only a small percentage of the adult male population has attended college, the question arises, how do many of the men from the lower levels use a college degree to get ahead? In brief, who gets educated today? And what is the meaning of this for the educational policy of our communities, for business enterprise, and for this country? For those men who think as business statesmen, or for those who plan a good competitive policy of personnel selection for the development of capable executives, the answer to this question is of vital importance: should we recruit and promote only college men or should we promote men from lesser ranks?

Chapter III, "The Royal Road: Higher Education," deals with these problems. It also discusses the colleges attended by successful men, those attended most frequently, and why the selection is made. Many of the business leaders went to Ivy League colleges. Others with a B.A. from a small college or a "cow college" move on to more prestigeful schools for higher degrees and for technical training to improve their chances for occupational advancement. What universities and graduate schools do they select, and what happens thereafter?

Successful men who climb to positions of power in Big Business cannot stand still. They are men in motion. There is not only "circulation of the elite" in the hierarchy of business and industry but movement back and forth throughout the forty-eight states. Some states and regions produce their share of leaders but lose them; other regions rear their own and acquire still more to help them solve their problems. In certain parts of the country, few future leaders are born, of whom many leave to go elsewhere, thus abandoning their birthplaces to men of possibly lesser stature and ability. The meaning of loss and gain of men of talent for the advancement and development of certain regions is of vital significance. The chapter called "Men in Motion: The Circulation of the Leaders" (IX) points out the facts and their meaning for the several regions of this country. It stresses the significance of spatial mobility in the lives of the men and their families, against a background of restlessness and movement over the nation. It tells the story of the immigrant and of the country boy migrating to the city. It shows how each goes through a process of learning and unlearning and of being acculturated and assimilated as he drives ahead toward power and esteem. Some of the case-history material illustrates how it is done and the price such men pay, which sometimes includes even rejection by their children.

The personalities of successful men, when related to their job performance, their past careers, their families, and what they do in their communities, are revealing. Some are men with capacities having no perceivable limits; their personal resources, their energy, intelligence, and inner well-being seem boundless. Others have no more than a bare minimum combination of the necessary characteristics to get by. Some are limited both for the job and the world beyond it. They are the narrow, shallow men whose presence at the top is sometimes a mystery to themselves and to their colleagues. Still others barely hold their jobs yet are successful socially, valued civic leaders, and important members of their local communities. Some men may be competent, skilled business leaders, with all the necessary business equipment, honest, loyal, and forever on the march, yet seemingly incapable of translating their moral and economic power into the rewards of family and community life. Eminently successful in business, admired and often envied, these men sometimes feel alone and frustrated, and wonder if "the price I paid got me anything I really wanted." Others, openly or covertly bitter and hostile, devote all their time to the job and assert "only my job matters, the hell with everything else." The chapters on the personalities of successful men examine their conscious and unconscious private worlds to learn how personality, and different kinds of personality, are related to the varying kinds of social and personal adjustment to jobs, families, and the world around them.

Earlier studies such as those of William E. Henry[2] show that there is at least one type of successful man who has been able to release himself from the close ties of his parental home. As an autonomous male, he can leave his father and, without unconscious hostility or resistance, relate his own fate with ease to other males in authority. Such men who "leave home" psychically are also freed from too close emotional ties to their mothers; while still loving and respecting both parents, they transfer their selves and their fates into other social contexts, including their businesses, where they can and do give the attention and energy necessary for solving present and immediate problems. The job, career, advancement, and the inner mental life of the man are given psychological analysis in the chapters about the private worlds of business leaders and the relation of personality to success and failure.

This discussion of American business leaders is based on the premise that, to understand the meaning of their careers, social as well as psychological evidence must be used. The whole man must be known and understood, including his rise from lower to

[2] William E. Henry, "The Business Executive: Psychodynamics of a Social Role," *American Journal of Sociology*, LIV (January, 1940), 286-91.

higher economic status, the development of his family and social life, as well as the person, the individual himself out of whom such a career unfolds. The personality studies of big business men are related to the larger survey of the career lines of men from all regions, from major industries and several positions in top management, to insure that the smaller group of men studied psychologically and individually are representative and characteristic of all business leaders in America.[3]

Although, in effect, this book implicitly is a "how-to-do-it" story, since it tells by example how and why thousands of business leaders rose to their present positions, Chapter X, "The Business World and the Business Career," deals more directly with this problem. It is *not* designed to give directives. Such is not our intent, nor is it within our capacity. Rather it shows how timing operates in job advancement, the life lines of the elite in the various industries, and the roles of expanding and static types of industry in the upward movement of a career. Profiles of the careers of successful men and excerpts from others are presented in several chapters to make more explicit the human significance of what we have said.

The meaning of Big Business Leadership for American life and a free interpretation of its significance are offered in the last chapter. The social meaning of occupational mobility in a flexible society and its meaning for democratic living are discussed there. The implications for free enterprise of the rewards of promotion and pay and of an open path for able men will be dealt with. The problems of promotion from within, the advancement of educated men from without, and the meaning of "blocked mobility" for those who have the ability and will to do but are prevented from achieving their ends by the enforcement of too rigid educational standards are discussed in the light of present evidence and the larger goal of our social and economic life. In

[3] W. Lloyd Warner and James Abegglen, *Occupational Mobility in American Business and Industry*, 1928-1952 (Minneapolis: University of Minnesota Press, 1955).

general, the last chapter deals with the significance of the evidence presented for the principles, precepts, and social implications of the good society.

Let us start in the next chapter by learning about the economic backgrounds of the families into which the future business leaders were born.

2
Leaders of Big Business:
A Birth and Mobile Class

The origins and careers of the men who direct American business bear directly on issues of profound importance to American society. Events of the past two decades have given rise to increasing concern on the part of Americans over their nation's well-being. In the face of ominous developments outside our country, reassuring comfort has been found in the vigor and resiliency of our domestic institutions and faiths, the belief in the right to obtain a good standard of living, to acquire stature in the community, and to accomplish this by individual determination and skill, with every man's chances what he alone makes them. These and companion beliefs have been called the American Dream, at the heart of which are two seemingly contradictory principles, apparently antithetical yet necessary to each other.

The first of these principles is the belief in equal opportunity—that every man, if he abides by the rules and is endowed with sufficient skill and determination, may aspire to the highest positions of the society. The second principle basic to our system, although less explicit in statement, is of unequal rank and status—that there is a social ladder, a ranking of the society's members. It is this ranking which defines the goals of equal opportunity, and this is the seeming paradox.

These beliefs constitute the reality of American democracy. Each is a necessary balance to the other. The principle of rank and status provides the motives for the maximal use of our

11

energies, for the orderly functioning of institutions, and for responsible leadership hierarchies.

The creed of equal opportunity is the indispensable opposing force against the power of social ranking, for rank and status orderings are necessary to the functioning of our complex society, but unrestrained development of them would reduce our society to a fixed order and destroy the present system of open classes with a chance for every man to achieve social movement upward. It is this opportunity for social mobility which gives meaning to the American Dream.

Is There More or Less Opportunity in America Today?

What is the present strength of these principles? If the belief in equal opportunity is indeed the central force in our democratic practices, the maintenance of these practices depends upon open classes and opportunities for social movement through individual effort and skill. When the man who equips himself with the requisite skills finds that his individual effort is no longer rewarded by movement, that the system is closing to him, and his is a futile endeavor, then other than democratic ways and beliefs may be sought to attain positions he expects access to. It is the responsibility of our democracy to examine itself and the forces that affect it and, if necessary, formulate social policy that will reaffirm its doctrines and revitalize its principles.

In our system of rank and status, no group is more important than the men who direct the vast economic enterprises that shape our lives. From a study of the origins of these men, it is possible to test in this critical area the reality now underlying the American Dream, the extent to which our society allows its members to shape their social destinies, and the degree to which the beliefs in equal opportunity are being supported. Executive positions in giant companies are the top for most men in our society; to what extent do men from all levels achieve these positions and is this opportunity increasing or decreasing?

To apply this critical test, the careers and backgrounds of more than eight thousand American business leaders were examined in this study. This group, as we said earlier, is made up of the men who lead the largest business firms in the country, selected to represent the wide range of types of business and industry in our economy. Not all American business leaders were included in the study, but all men included are business leaders, and they represent the highest positions in the largest companies in all types of American enterprise.[1]

By studying the backgrounds and careers of these men, it is possible to see the social movement and life chances in this important area of our society. To the extent that the men who direct American business are the sons and grandsons of business leaders, our social system may be said to be closed, for to that extent the higher positions in our economic system are available only to those whose families have power and prestige. To the extent that the leaders of American business are men who have come from factory, farm, shop, and office backgrounds, the American Dream of equal opportunity for all men from all ranks is being realized.

Is it possible to say today that every man's chances are as good as the next man's in American business? Is movement possible from lower social positions to high rank, income, and prestige? These questions probe the values, beliefs, and ideals of our society; in the answers, as shown in this study, lies a measure of the vigor and endurance of our democratic practices.

Furthermore, by comparing the present-day business leaders with those of a generation ago, it is possible to examine the deep and continuing trends of our society. If now there is movement of men from all levels of our system into the business elite, has freedom of social movement and social advance increased or decreased? Is the Dream increasingly realized, with more men moving from all backgrounds into the powerful positions of business leadership; or is the Dream fading, as the social system becomes more rigid and men are compelled to remain in the ranks to which they were

[1] See Warner and Abegglen, *op. cit.*, for a detailed statement of the methods and techniques employed in the study.

born? The comparison of the business elite of 1928 with the results of the study of 1952 will make it possible to answer these crucial questions.

Where Do Our Business Leaders Come From?

The men who hold the top positions in American business today are in most cases from the higher levels of American society. Slightly over half are sons of owners or executives of business firms, and 14 per cent the sons of professional men—sons of doctors, engineers, ministers, lawyers, teachers, or men in other professional occupations. Thus two of every three leaders of American business come from families whose economic and social positions were well above the average for the nation.

The remaining third of the business elite are primarily from white-collar and laboring backgrounds, a smaller proportion from farm backgrounds, and only a few from other occupations— military service, political and governmental careers, and so forth (see Chart I).

Whatever our national hopes, the business leaders of America are a select group, drawn for the most part from the upper ranks. Only to a limited extent may it be said that every man's chances are as good as the next man's, for birth in the higher occupational levels improves these life chances considerably. If equal opportunity were realized in practice, the business elite and the nation as a whole would share a common background, whereas the composition of the business elite is clearly weighted toward the higher occupational levels of our society.

For a more precise measure of opportunity for men from different occupational origins, the business elite was compared with the whole population for proportions of men from each type of background. If "equal opportunity" were a reality, and social background had no relation to the position a man occupies at the culmination of his career, the proportion of sons of laborers or of white-collar workers in the business elite would be the same as in the nation as a whole, and so on for all occupations. In other words,

if men's careers were not shaped by their social backgrounds and
if they could advance in business without being influenced by their
fathers' positions, the social backgrounds of men at all levels
(including the business elite) would approximate the general
population. An exact measurement of the mobility chances for

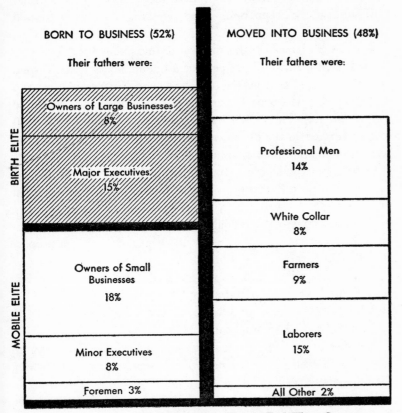

BORN TO BUSINESS (52%)

Their fathers were:

MOVED INTO BUSINESS (48%)

Their fathers were:

BIRTH ELITE

Owners of Large Businesses
8%

Major Executives
15%

Professional Men
14%

White Collar
8%

MOBILE ELITE

Owners of Small
Businesses
18%

Minor Executives
8%

Farmers
9%

Laborers
15%

Foremen 3%

All Other 2%

Chart I.   From What Economic Levels Did They Come?

men from each type of background can be made by comparing
the occupations of their fathers with the occupations of the adult
male population in 1920.

The occupations of the fathers of the business leaders studied
were given on the questionnaires for the time the business leaders

became self-supporting, which was, on the average, at about twenty. Since their average present age is fifty-three, the information on the occupations of their fathers is given for about thirty-three years ago, or around the time of the 1920 census.

This measure takes account of the great changes in occupations —the reduction in number of farmers, the increase in white-collar and professional occupations—that our economy has witnessed in the past half century.

As an example of how this method of measuring our democratic practice works, since 47 per cent of all adult males in 1920 were laborers, it would be expected that, given equal movement into top business positions, about 47 per cent of the business elite would be sons of laborers. The mobility rate in this case would be 100—100 sons of laborers in the business elite for every 100 expected on the basis of population figures. If more than 47 per cent of the business elite were sons of laborers, then laboring backgrounds would be overrepresented in the business elite and the mobility rate would be more than 100. In actual fact, only 15 per cent of the present-day business leaders are sons of laborers; only 32 sons of laborers become business leaders out of every 100 expected from the proportion in the general population.

Three occupations make up a larger share of business leadership than their share of the population would indicate. The mobility rate for sons of owners of small business is 360, of professional men, 350, of foremen, 133.

The men whose fathers were laborers, white-collar workers, or farmers all appear in the business elite in smaller proportions than their share of the population.

The mobility rate for sons of unskilled or semi-skilled laborers is 16 to 100; for sons of farmers, 40 to 100; sons of skilled laborers, 63; white-collar workers most nearly approach equal and proportionate representation with a ratio of 80. These groups make up about 85 per cent of the population but only a third of the nation's business leaders.

These comparisons of the business elite with the population are the test of the extent to which it may be said that all men, regardless of their origins, move into all levels of the business system. The disparities are enormous. The sons of farm laborers at one extreme are almost entirely absent from the business elite, contrasted with sons of big business men who occupy nearly eight

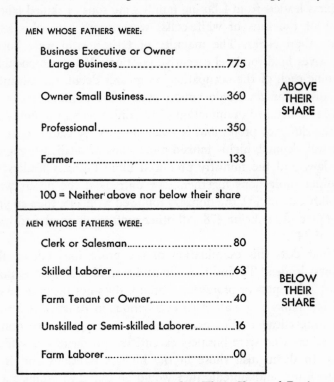

MEN WHOSE FATHERS WERE:

Business Executive or Owner
  Large Business.................................775

Owner Small Business.......................360

Professional......................................350

Farmer...133

ABOVE
THEIR
SHARE

100 = Neither above nor below their share

MEN WHOSE FATHERS WERE:

Clerk or Salesman............................ 80

Skilled Laborer.................................63

Farm Tenant or Owner...................... 40

Unskilled or Semi-skilled Laborer.............16

Farm Laborer...................................00

BELOW
THEIR
SHARE

Chart II.   What Occupations Get Their Share of Business Leadership?[a]

[a] This chart shows how various occupations are represented among the origins of the business leaders. For example, if an occupation has 10 per cent in the general population and the same percentage of business leaders it scores 100; if less among the leaders, under 100; if more, over.

times their proportionate share of elite positions. These differences are shown in Chart II.

Even these measures underestimate the great differences in occupational mobility. The occupational groups are broad, and each includes many levels of occupational positions. For example, farm backgrounds include a range of social positions from small tenant farmers to owners of great ranches and agricultural empires. Most of the business elite who come from farm backgrounds are sons of the owners and managers of large farms. The majority of business leaders from laboring families are sons of skilled laborers. Most of the sons of white-collar workers are sons of salesmen rather than clerks. The majority of fathers who were business executives held top-level executive positions. If it were possible to examine each of the occupations in greater detail, the advantages and disadvantages would appear even more pronounced.

A more detailed examination of the differences in mobility rates for the different professions is made possible by census data. The four well-defined, highly ranked professions of medicine, engineering, law, and the ministry produced more business leaders than all other professions together. Law outranked the others with a mobility rate of 800, the ministry followed with 548, then engineering 480, and medicine 478. All other professions combined have a rate of 148.

What does this examination of the professions tell us about business leaders? To find that the background of lawyer outranked all other business or professional groups does not mean necessarily that law ranks above all other occupations in America as a source of business leaders. For example, if it were possible to examine the fathers who were business executives and owners in sufficient detail to distinguish those in the highest positions and in the largest firms, undoubtedly they would be found to produce a still higher proportion of business leaders than do lawyers. This high mobility of lawyers' sons into the highest levels of business means that within each of the general types of occupations there are further extremes of advantage and disadvantage in business mobility.

In addition, the practice of these professions, and law in particular, confers on their members a substantial place in the community. Those fathers in the more solid professions achieve in most cases a high level of prestige, income, and style of life. Their sons are trained as desirable members of society. Their families meet and know the other community leaders. The sons of professional men expect to attend and complete college, and in most cases take advanced training; they marry the daughters of important men in the community. These and the many other advantages held by the sons of professional men are all reflected in their high proportion in the business elite. Moreover, the close relations between the great law firms and large corporations, and between legal and business training, all add to the advantage held by sons of lawyers in moving into the highest levels of American business.

Grandfathers, Fathers, and Business Leadership

The central question for this study is, what is the present reality underlying the American Dream of equal opportunity? From the evidence presented, the answer would be largely negative and pessimistic. Before attempting such a reckoning, however, the business leaders and their backgrounds must be seen in a larger social view. The problem has been approached, up to this point, by comparing the positions of the men of the business elite with those of their fathers, and comparing this in turn with the nation as a whole.

In this approach, social mobility is measured by the changes taking place from the position of the father to the position of the son. This is only part of the meaning of social mobility, for the movement of men into the business elite does not always take place in a single generation. The men we have seen moving into high positions from laboring and clerical backgrounds do indeed make the long jump in their own careers, but the arrival of most of the men in their present high and powerful positions represents the culmination of several generations of social movement. Their careers are the result of a series of social changes that have taken place over the generations, the careers of the grandfathers and fathers combining with their own efforts to result finally in an elite position in present-day business.

The occupations of the grandfathers and fathers of the business leaders are shown in Chart III, with the changes between the two generations. While half of the fathers of the present business leaders were business men—owners or executives—only a third of the grandfathers were business men. While nearly 7 out of 10 of the fathers were professional or business men, only 4 out of 10 of the grandfathers were in these higher-level occupations and more were laborers. Underlying these changes is the fact that

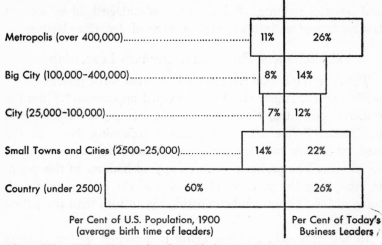

	Per Cent of U.S. Population, 1900 (average birth time of leaders)	Per Cent of Today's Business Leaders
Metropolis (over 400,000)	11%	26%
Big City (100,000–400,000)	8%	14%
City (25,000–100,000)	7%	12%
Small Towns and Cities (2500–25,000)	14%	22%
Country (under 2500)	60%	26%

Chart III.   Who Were the Grandfathers and Fathers of Successful Men?

less than one in ten of the fathers were farmers, compared with over a third of the grandfathers.

The question of opportunity and social movement is complex. Mobility into the business elite is a continuing process, one which occurs over several generations and cannot be seen merely as the change in occupation from father to son. When it is seen in this broader context, the great currents of movement in our nation show up in sharp profile. Few of the business leaders were sons of farmers, but over a third were the grandsons of farmers—the movement from the farm to the business leadership spans a social distance not usually traversed in one generation. A few men born on the farm do achieve business leadership; typically, however, the son of a farmer makes the move from farm to city, becoming a laborer or white-collar worker in most cases, a professional man in a few. It is the grandson of the farmer whom we find in the business elite.

If we look further at the broader sweep of social mobility as shown by the changes in occupation from grandfather to business leader, we find not only these men on the move but their families as well. The change from grandfather's occupation to father's occupation is an upward one. The proportion of big business men in the second generation doubles the proportion of grandfathers who were major executives or large owners, and the proportion in the professions increases by nearly 50 per cent. The movement between the generations is not only from the farm to the city but upward on the social ladder.

The changes in occupation from grandfather to father to son take place in broad patterns traced with channels of movement. As the fathers of the men in the business elite moved from the farms to the city, many entered laboring occupations, and a substantial group entered the professions, no doubt in part as a result of the rise of the great state universities during this period, as they provided financial and geographic access to professional training for farm youth in the Midwest especially. Indeed, sons of farmers moved into nearly all occupational groups in considerable numbers, except top business positions, a move delayed until the next generation. Thus, movement from the farm to business leadership is almost entirely a three-generational process, taking place through the entire occupational system.

The cases where the grandfather was a laborer present a more restricted pattern. In the father's generation, movement took place from the shop and factory into white-collar work at the lower levels, for the most part; in the next generation, the move was completed to business leadership.

Small business and white-collar occupations seem to be pivot points in the systems of movement. There is a good deal of interchange between these groups from one generation to the next, as the fathers of business leaders from each of these backgrounds moved into the other in large numbers, along with men from laboring and farm backgrounds. Just as these occupations generally occupy lower-middle-class rank in the social-class system, so they appear to be a middle ground in the inter-generational mobility of families to business leadership.

This is the evidence on which to examine the present state of the American Dream, the facts about opportunity and social movement into the top ranks of American business. The origins of the business elite have been presented, and the proportions of business leaders from each occupational group compared with the proportions if social movement and social rank were not connected. A broader view of the process of social movement has been seen, as it affects the life-chances of Americans in business.

Is opportunity a reality in American business? The evidence does not allow a simple answer. Some men from all levels of the occupational system achieve top ranking positions in the largest American businesses. Business leaders include sons of laborers, sons of farmers, and sons of white-collar workers. The American system of rank is not a closed system, with its highest positions available only to the well-born, for it allows men from all backgrounds to enter its elite.

This is the first answer to the question of opportunity in America. It is only a small part of the answer. Overriding these facts of freedom of social movement are the facts of privilege and advantage. The great majority of business leaders are sons of men who were in the higher occupational levels. The proportion of men from these backgrounds in the business elite exceeds many-fold their proportion in the total population. Great disparities in social movement exist, for the proportion of men in business leadership from each of the occupational groups increases with the rank of that group. The American system of rank is by no means an open one, and movement upward is closely related to birth position and family prestige.

However, when social movement in American business is seen in its larger context, taking place over several generations, the tremendous sweep of change in social position is revealed over the entire nation. Few business leaders represent several generations of elite position. The social movement into business leadership does not usually take place in a single generation. But when seen in this larger span of social time, change not stability, flexibility not rigidity are the underlying reality.

The Business Leaders of Today and Yesterday

The full meaning of these facts about mobility in America today can be understood only when they are viewed against some realistic standard. We have compared the amount of opportunity represented in business today with an "ideal" standard, and measured the system as it is actually working against the "ideal" conditions of a completely free and open society. We have found that our business system is far from realizing this ideal and to a considerable extent it may be said that ours is a closed society. Far more evidence of birth privilege and social rigidity has been found than would exist were the dream of equal opportunity being realized.

Does this evidence force upon us the conclusion that our system is failing in its efforts to realize its ideals—that the American Dream is only a dream and cannot be realized? A less arduous measure of the effectiveness of our system is a comparison of today with the past. Is mobility increasing or decreasing? Does this system, admittedly imperfect as it now functions, allow increasing freedom of social rank, or is the system closing, becoming more rigid, and failing to use all of its individuals effectively?

When Americans consider their history, and how the society functioned in past generations to provide opportunities for its men, a whole series of persons and events call to mind vast opportunities and spectacular successes: the frontier, Lincoln, the immigrants, Andrew Carnegie, the Alger heroes—a parade of places and persons each expressing the freedom, opportunity, and equality of the society, and each telling a story of successful accomplishment in a nation where all men are born equal. The image of the national past is of a time when men were able to shape their destinies in the expanding, less complex, more democratic communities of our fathers, unhampered by the social and economic barriers we encounter in our present-day careers.

These powerful legends, when compared with the difficult and prosaic reality of the present, create a disposition to pessimism and doubt about the American Dream. Mobility is believed to be diminishing, and influence, family connections, and the other elements of birth position to be increasing in importance in business careers. In fact, it is doubtful that such an open and fluid society as the legends describe ever did exist; the most precise evidence now available indicates that the men who directed American business during the nineteenth and early twentieth centuries were with some few spectacular exceptions the products of the higher social and economic levels of their day. The legendary image of the past persists, however, powerfully nourished by nostalgia, and both layman and social scientist use it as the yardstick to measure the present.

An examination of the business elite of one generation ago is available. A comparison of the two periods should indicate the direction our society is taking. In 1928 F. W. Taussig and C. S. Joslyn surveyed the social origins of the business leaders of that time.[2] Their study is a landmark in its field, and the authors' care and completeness in reporting their methods and results provide the basis for a precise answer to the question of the trends in our business system.

Before the results of the earlier study are examined, and the past compared with the present, the time periods should be fixed in mind. The business leaders of 1928, like those of 1952, were studied as the economy reached a peak of expansion. Therefore, in this respect the periods are generally comparable. In the period since the 1928 study, an interval of about one generation, the nation has

[2] Taussig and Joslyn, *op. cit.*

experienced a major depression, a major war, and a period of substantial economic expansion. The similarities and differences between the two eras are indeed a measure of the long-range trends of our society.

To make the comparison of the two periods accurate, the methods and techniques of the study of the present-day business leaders were made comparable in every way possible with those of the earlier study. At both times, the men studied were from the highest levels of American business, the top executives and owners of the largest companies in our economy, representing the full range of types of commerce and industry and all parts of the nation.

TABLE I.   THE ORIGINS OF BUSINESS LEADERS OF 1928 AND 1952
(*in percentages*)

Occupation of Father	1928	1952	1928-1952 Difference
Unskilled or semi-skilled laborer	2	5	3
Skilled laborer	9	10	1
Clerk or salesman	5	8	3
Minor executive	7	11	4
Major executive	17	15	−2
Owner small business	20	18	−2
Owner large business	14	8	−6
Professional	13	14	1
Farmer	12	9	−3
Other	1	2	1
Total	100	100	

Who were the business leaders of 1928 and how do they compare in social origins with those of the present day? Table I presents a detailed comparison of the two periods and the differences between them. The overall difference is clear. *The present-day business leadership includes more men from the lower-level occupations.* While both in 1928 and in 1952 most business leaders are sons of business men, the proportion is smaller now than a generation ago.

To take up the differences between the two periods in detail, it will be remembered that sons of laborers, sons of white-collar workers, and sons of farmers are under-represented among present-day business leaders, occupying only a third of the top business positions. However, a generation ago these men held an even smaller proportion of the top positions. The proportion of sons of unskilled or semi-skilled laborers in business leadership has more than doubled in the interval, the proportion of sons of skilled laborers has increased, and that of sons of white-collar workers has nearly doubled. Of all the under-represented social groups, only sons of farmers make up a smaller proportion of the business leaders today.

Among the other occupational groups, sons of business and professional men, the opposite pattern generally holds. The proportion of sons of business owners, large and small, has declined considerably, from about a third of the 1928 business leaders to about a quarter of the present day. Sons of major executives make up a smaller proportion of the present-day leadership and sons of professional men about the same proportion.

Just as the occupations of the fathers of the business leaders of today were compared with the occupations of the population in 1920 to measure mobility, so the occupations of the fathers of the 1928 business leaders must be compared with the occupations of the population in 1900. From the comparison it is possible to obtain the rates of mobility for both generations and measure accurately changes in rates of mobility for each occupational group.[3]

Moreover, these differences in the social origins of the business leaders of today and a generation ago must be evaluated in light of the broader changes in our economy during this period. For example, we find that fewer sons of farmers are top business leaders today than a generation earlier. Since the proportion of farmers in the population has decreased from 1900 to 1920, this change in the proportion of sons of farmers in the business elite

---

[3] Since the 1900 census reports are much less complete than more recent ones, the comparison between mobility rates for 1928 and the present must be limited to five occupational groups: laborers, clerks and salesmen, business owners and executives, professional men, and farmers.

might simply be a result of the decreasing number of farmers. Similarly for other occupations. Three groups increased in proportion of the population from 1900 to 1920—white-collar workers, professional men, and business men. The proportion of sons in the business elite increased from 1928 to 1952 for two of these, white-collar workers and professional men.

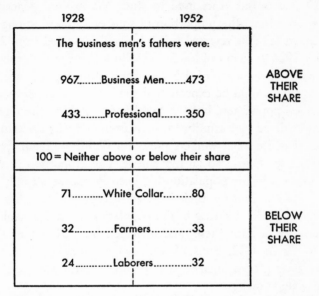

	1928	1952	
The business men's fathers were:			
967........Business	Men.......473		ABOVE THEIR SHARE
433........Professional........350			
100 = Neither above or below their share			
71..........White	Collar.........80		BELOW THEIR SHARE
32............Farmers............33			
24............Laborers...........32			

Chart IV.   Who Got Their Share in 1928 and 1952?[a]

[a] Those occupations above 100 have a higher percentage of business leaders than their percentages in the general population of America; those below have a smaller percentage.

The question becomes one of the extent to which the change in the makeup of the business elite simply reflects broader changes in the whole population, and the extent to which these are real changes in the amount of mobility that is taking place.

More or Less Opportunity Today?

The mobility rates for 1928 and 1952 are shown in Chart IV. Without exception, those occupations that have less than their proportionate share of elite positions in 1952 were at an even greater disadvantage in 1928. The mobility rates for sons of laborers, white-collar workers, and farmers were even lower in 1928 than they are today. Men from factory, office, shop, and farm backgrounds are now able in greater numbers to achieve top-level positions in American business than a generation ago.

The proportion of laborers in the population declined from 1900 to 1920, the census years used to study the fathers' generations. At the same time, the proportion of sons of laborers among business leaders actually reversed this trend and increased from 24 out of 100 in 1928 to 32 out of 100 in 1952. Both today and a generation ago, many fewer sons of laborers reach the top of American business than would be expected on the basis of their proportions in the total population, but the trend is definitely in the direction of more realized opportunity for men from laboring backgrounds.

Sons of white-collar workers present a slightly different pattern of increase in upward social movement. The proportion of white-collar workers in the population has been increasing steadily since the turn of the century; their increase in elite positions has more than balanced this increase in the population, with the result that the mobility rate for these men increased from 71 out of 100 in 1928 to 80 in 1952. Sons of white-collar workers more nearly achieve their proportionate share of top business positions today than a generation ago.

Like white-collar workers, the professional group in America has been increasing over the past several decades and their proportion of business leaders has increased during the past 25 years. However, unlike the case of the white-collar group, the sons of professional men have not kept pace in terms of upper echelon business positions with their increase in the population. The mobility rate for sons of professional men of 433 to 100 in 1928, or over four times their proportionate share of top business positions, has diminished to 350.

The crux of the problem of inheritance and mobility, of course, is the mobility rate for sons of business men today and a generation ago; it is here that the greatest change has taken place. The population change from 1900 to 1920 in the proportion of business executives and owners was toward greater numbers, from about 1 in 20 to about 1 in 10. However, the share of the business elite held by sons of business men reversed this population trend, as their proportions decreased from 58 per cent in 1928 to 52 per cent in 1952. Expressed in terms of mobility rate, this was a decline from 967, or nearly ten times their population proportion, to 473, or less than five times their population proportion.

Only in the case of sons of farmers has there been little or no change in mobility into the business elite. The 1928 study of business leaders pointed up the limited movement of farmers' sons into business leadership. Since that time, with an enormous increase in transportation and communication facilities, the isolation of farmers and their families from the larger American society has been much reduced. There are fewer social differences in education, habits, and style of life between city and rural residents, and these differences are being continually lessened. Also, during the generation under study, many farmers and their families moved to the cities, and sons of farmers were forced by circumstances if not by choice to turn to the cities for jobs, increasing their numbers in the urban job markets, and placing them in geographic positions, at least, to move to business leadership.

It might be expected that the mobility rate of sons of farmers would increase from 1928 to 1952 along with the rates for sons of laborers and white-collar workers. However, the low rate of mobility into top business positions for sons of farmers generally continues at the present time. Despite the fact that there has been a trend to greater representation in the business elite of men from the disadvantaged groups in the population, 1928 and 1952 present a similar picture for sons of farmers. The mobility rate of 32 out of every 100 expected in 1928 stands in 1952 at 33 out of every 100, evidence that the process of mobility from farm to business leadership is largely a three-generation cycle, from grandfather to father to son.

This comparison of American business of one generation ago

with American business today provides the basis for an accurate answer to the questions raised about the direction in which our social system is traveling. There is no doubt that both in the 1920's and in the 1950's birth conferred great advantages on business careers. In both periods, the proportions of sons of professional and business men in the elite greatly exceed their proportions in the population. During both periods, some men from all levels achieve business leadership, but relatively few sons of farmers, laborers, clerks, or salesmen actually climb to the top of our business system. The Dream is far from reality, both yesterday and today.

However, it is no less true, and far more important, that the system is increasingly open to men from the lower occupational ranks. Not only is there no evidence that opportunity for sons of farmers, laborers, and white-collar workers is decreasing, but movement from these backgrounds into the business elite takes place in greater degree today than a generation ago. The system is not closing and becoming more rigid—in fact, it is more flexible and increasingly recruits its leaders from all parts of our society.

These changes can be expressed more generally. From 1900 to 1920 the occupations of laborer, farmer, and white-collar worker in the population *decreased 7 per cent*. From 1928 to 1952 the proportion of business leaders from these backgrounds *increased 5 per cent*. On the other hand, the population proportions of business and professional men *increased 7 per cent*, while their share of business leadership from 1928 to 1952 *decreased 5 per cent*. In other words, while more men were sons of business and professional men, fewer business leaders were drawn from this group; although fewer men were sons of laborers, white-collar workers, and farmers, more of the business elite were drawn from these backgrounds.

There is additional evidence from the study of the business leaders that freedom and flexibility of social position are increasing in American business. The extreme of social inheritance in business is found in those cases where the son of a business leader not only becomes a business leader himself but also holds his position in the same firm that his father directed. The son not only has an equivalent business rank but holds a rank at least outwardly identical with that of his father. This extreme type of rigidity and social inheritance took place in 14 per cent of the cases studied in 1928 and in only 9 per cent in 1952.

Increased mobility into higher level positions is not a temporary or newly won gain in social freedom. The trend to greater social flexibility is also apparent when the business leaders of 1952 are followed back through the grandfather's generation, and the patterns compared with those of the 1928 business elite. More of the grandfathers of the 1952 business leaders were laborers and fewer were business executives or owners than the grandfathers of the 1928 business elite. Moreover, a larger proportion of the fathers of 1952 business leaders entered a different occupation from that of the grandfathers. In general, the channels of movement from occupation of grandfather to father were the same for the two time periods. The important difference between the two generations preceding the elite groups of 1928 and 1952 is that the fathers of the 1952 group, like their sons, more often came from lower-status occupational backgrounds, and moved in larger numbers to higher occupational levels than did the fathers of the 1928 group. Increased mobility has taken place not only in the lifetimes of present-day business leaders but in the careers of their fathers as well.

Business Leaders: 1900 to 1950

To sketch out on an even broader canvas the direction our society is taking in the kinds of men who lead its business enterprises, it is possible to estimate the social origins of business leaders for about 1900, 1920, 1930, and 1950, and to plot the trends in the recruitment of the business leaders through these periods.

The fathers of the 1928 business leaders who were themselves major business executives or owners of large businesses provide a selection of business leaders for the period around 1900. The fathers of the 1952 business leaders who were major executives or owners of large businesses form a similar group for the period around 1920. The 1928 business elite provide a basis for estimating the origins of the business elite around 1930, and the decade beginning in 1950 may be represented by the men studied in 1952. Thus a sampling of the business leadership of America over half a century is available, including in the 1900 group men born before the Civil War, whose careers were worked out in the period of our nation's greatest expansion, through the turbulent decades leading to the present.

These four groups are not entirely comparable, of course. The 1930 and 1950 business leaders are a careful selection from the top of the American business system. The 1900 and 1920 groups probably include more men who were with smaller businesses, and men of lesser positions. Because their business positions were at a somewhat lower level, there would probably be more men of lower-level backgrounds included in these two groups, and they should, therefore, make for a conservative estimate of the amount of occupational inheritance during the two periods of 1900 and 1920.

Nevertheless, when the four periods are examined, there is confirmation of the long-term, continuing trend to greater realization of opportunity in American business and to an increase in the proportion of men from the "bottom" who make their way to the "top." As shown in Table II, the proportion of sons of laborers in top-level business positions increases steadily over the half century, nearly doubling from 1900 to 1950. Paralleling their increase in the population, the proportion of sons of white-collar workers in business leadership more than triples during this period. As for the sons of professional men, the proportion moving into business leadership has increased, as has their proportion of the population, but the increase in business elite representation has not been great.

The sons of owners of small business have comprised about the

TABLE II.   LONG-RANGE TRENDS IN MOBILITY IN AMERICAN BUSINESS
(*in percentages*)

Occupational Origins of the Leaders	1900[a]	1920[a]	1930[a]	1950[a]	1900-1950 Difference
White collar	5	7	12	19	14
Laborer	7	10	11	15	8
Professional	11	10	13	14	3
Major executives	15	13	17	15	0
Owner small business	19	23	20	18	−1
Owner large business	17	16	14	8	−9
Farmer	24	21	12	9	−15
Other	2	0	1	2	0
Total	100	100	100	100	

[a] Dates are approximate

same proportion of business leadership throughout the half century, and the same has been true for sons of major business executives. However, the proportion of sons of owners of large businesses has diminished considerably, from 17 per cent in 1900 to only 8 per cent at the present time. The sons of farmers have also declined in business elite representation. In 1900 nearly a quarter of all business leaders were farmers' sons, compared with only one tenth in 1950. This decrease parallels their decrease in the total population.

In the longest view possible, all evidence indicates that in American society opportunity continues to be realized, and increasingly so. Rather than closing in on men of low birth, holding them to the positions into which they were born, our social system continues to make it possible for men from all levels to move into elite positions in commerce and industry.

3

The Royal Road:
Higher Education

The Educated Many and the Uneducated Few

One of the fundamental tenets of our early democracy that has persisted through the development of our nation is the right of the individual to equal opportunity. One reason that this principle has survived in *fact*, in spite of the many fictions around it, is that we have provided the opportunity for higher education to almost all who would seek it and have the capacity to profit by it. Because of the value placed upon education, the demand for it, the recognition given to it, the opportunity to get an advanced education has become one of the great equalizing forces in our social system.

Not everyone has the capacity to profit by this opportunity; not everyone has the motivating drive to take advantage of it. But formal education has increased for the general population. It has increased in much greater proportions among the men who are the present heads of our large corporations. Three fourths of these men at least attended college, over half of all of them graduated, and a third of these went on to postgraduate work. This leaves only one fourth of the total group who did not go to college.

Comparing the business leaders with the general population shows that the great differences lie at the extremes (see Chart V). Since the fact that it is possible for many people to get a college education at public expense should be an equalizing factor, we wonder what is involved in the lives and personalities of the business leaders that will motivate them to get college degrees in

34

eight times the proportion of the general population. Are they the sons of business leaders and the sons of college men?

At the other extreme, it is of equal interest that there is so large a group that achieved business success with no college education at all. What kinds of men were these who could achieve the

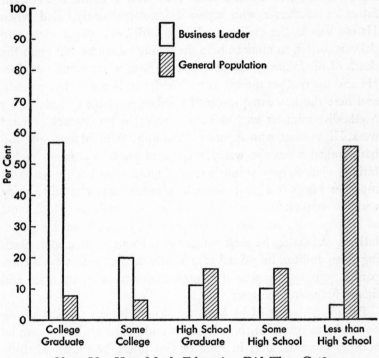

Chart V.   How Much Education Did They Get?

highest positions in American business and industry without the equipment of a formal education? What kinds of families did they come from, what regions, what communities? Were they perhaps forced to go to work at an early age to support the family and, finally, through perseverance and a driving motivation and innate ability—and some luck—achieve business success? Were some, at least, the sons of well-established business leaders who followed the tradition that the business itself was the best training ground for their sons?

The Mobile Elite Tell What Education Means to Them

Harold Palmer, the senior officer in a large nation-wide distributing company, grew up in a small town near Wichita, Kansas. His father, a mechanic who repaired farm machinery, died when Harold was in the eighth grade. He had had a paper route and delivery jobs in summer to help the family's finances, but upon the death of his father it was necessary for him to get a full-time job. He and his mother moved into Wichita to live with her parents, and here the boy came under the influence of his grandfather, a Methodist minister with a strong belief in the virtues of hard work. His mother, who apparently was quite talented musically and had studied when she was younger and played the organ in her father's church, gave piano lessons. Harold, who has always loved music and finds it a great source of pleasure now, wanted to study with his mother; but his job as a helper on a milk route took most of his daytime hours and, in the evening, largely upon his grandfather's insistence, he took courses at a commercial school. Starting as an auditor, he gained valuable experience with several companies, joining his present organization several years later and finally becoming treasurer.

Palmer is impressed by his own success, by the number of big names he associates with in business and in the philanthropies he actively supports. But, in spite of this pride, he thinks wistfully about his lack of formal education. "I was crazy about school. I was simply heartbroken about not going to college. I didn't go because of finances. I've been associated all of my life with college men. I've always felt that it has been a personal loss to me that I didn't go to college. Maybe that's why I want my son to graduate from college."

As the son of a skilled laborer, Palmer represents the small proportion (9 per cent) of that, or any, occupational group of men whose sons had less than high school education, yet somehow moved into the positions of prestige and power occupied by our business elite. The proportions of those having less than high school, or only some high school, are highest (14 per cent) for the lowest-status occupational category and lowest (1 per cent) for the occupational groups of high status.

Palmer revealed that he has good relations with the people around him in his organization, likes to look after able men under him who need help and encouragement, indicating a degree of security that makes this possible; but he feels a lack of security with those he considers his social and business superiors. He has channeled all of his training and efforts into the financial stream, becoming expert in this one field of business management and a valuable officer and board member of his firm on matters of fiscal policy. But the intensity with which he has concentrated his efforts and the limitations on his social and cultural interests have cut him off from a social group, except in philanthropies where his function again is largely financial.

Another member of the business leaders who, like Palmer, had less than high school education, is a man who meets and entertains big-name people every day with complete aplomb and certainly no evidence of Palmer's awe in associating with prestige-ful names. He too, however, feels a loss in his lack of formal education. "I often feel the lack of education, particularly in the past. Even now I wonder if I am expressing myself properly; sometimes I can forget it, and talk a lot; other times I just sit among a lot of degrees and listen. I still get butterflies in my stomach when I'm to make a speech, but it seems I do better when I don't prepare them." Unlike Palmer this is a man who has always read a great deal, especially about certain people in history who have engaged his interest. The volumes in his library have been chosen with great care and, although most of the books are beautifully bound, one does not feel that any of them are there simply as decoration. As a sign of culture?—in part, perhaps yes.

The books seem to share a place of equal interest with photographs of famous persons whom this man has known and entertained—people in government, in business, in the literary world, in entertainment. He enjoys calling them by their first names and in other ways indicating social and intellectual intimacy. All of this indicates that here is a man who has developed broad career lines involving social and cultural interest in spite of his limited education.

We have been talking about the small group of men of low occupational background who reached the top without the advantage of a college education—and did it the hard way. But over half of the business leaders born to skilled or unskilled laborers went to college or graduated. This proportion increases steadily as one proceeds up the occupational scale: three fourths of the sons of small owners, almost that proportion of the sons of white-collar workers and of farmers, nine of ten of the sons of big business and professional men had some college work or graduated.

An important fact to be noticed here is that all levels of occupational background, from unskilled worker to the big business owner and professional man, had more sons who were college graduates than in any other educational category. Also, as the level of educational achievement declines (from college graduate to less than high school) the percentages are reduced rapidly for every group but the unskilled workers.

One might infer from this that the men who make up our business leadership have been motivated to achievement throughout their careers, that they were ambitious to get an education, whether it was easy or not, and that this ambition continued to drive them on to higher and higher goals in the business world. An indication that this may be so is in the fact that so many of those who started college went on to finish: of those who started, only one fourth did not graduate.

Most of the men born to high occupational position went to college as a matter of course, usually to the college of their fathers and perhaps the same preparatory school as well. Many of them were serious scholars, considered teaching, did graduate work here and abroad. However, a very small proportion, 12 per cent, of business leaders whose fathers, and perhaps grandfathers, occupied high positions in the business world, were not educated beyond high school. Since being born to position does not by any means assure one's staying there, how did it happen that these men, born at the top, did not take advantage of the education they so easily could have had, and what did this do to their career stories?

William Reeves, a youthful president of a wholesale grocery chain that had been started and built by his father into a nation-wide organization, talked about his education: "Father didn't care one way or the other about my going to college, but he felt very strongly that I had to stay in school until I had met college entrance requirements. Neither he nor my mother went to college.

"I was very strongly influenced by my father. We had a farm where we raised a lot of stuff, and that's where I learned to ride and hunt. Those are the pleasantest memories I have. I always get a thrill from working the dogs, and to develop the ability of the dogs to handle the birds was fun. Besides, I like to be in the woods."

The only childhood worries that Reeves recalls now revolved around staying in school. "I was lousy. But my sister was good. She was better than my brother and I put together. I had a hell of a time just staying in it. I never could do languages at all because you couldn't prove it. Besides I was always wondering how many covey of quail I could uncover down on the ranch or why one puppy was better than another when I should have been thinking about my schoolwork."

Now Reeves feels that what he should have done was to go to agricultural college for two years, not so much to make him a better business executive but because "agriculture is the backbone of this country." He has a farm, where he lives and commutes to the city. He raises and trains hunters and is master of hounds for the local hunt. There is no evidence that he regrets not having gone on to a conventional liberal arts degree, nor does he express any inadequacy in his ability to conduct the business or in his social relations because of it. His high social position from birth and the kind of life he has had because of it account for this contrast between him and his less secure counterparts who originated from low-status occupational backgrounds.

Among the birth elite, 18 per cent had some college but did not graduate. Seventy per cent of this group graduated.

We have been looking at the extremes in education and effort: the man who came from the bottom of the heap and, with no education beyond high school, got to the top; the man born to the top who did not take advantage of the education he easily could have had, yet stayed in the place of his birth. Stories of other business leaders could be told—less dramatic often, but more representative. Among the occupational groups between the bottom and the top are varied histories: many families at these levels could afford to send their sons to college or at least to aid them substantially, and some of the boys were good students or outstanding in other respects and received scholarships. The stories have as many variations as individuals, of course, but the theme that holds throughout is the drive to achievement.

The Education of the Business Leaders' Fathers

It might well be assumed that college-educated fathers would always see to it that they had college-educated sons and that fathers at lower levels of education would have sons of higher educational achievement than they, given the fact that these are ambitious sons. We have just seen that the sons of all occupational levels were highly represented as college graduates, but we have not had the opportunity to see the relation between the education of the fathers and the education of the sons.

Whereas over half of the sons had graduated from college, over half of the fathers had only some high school, or less than high school, education. The two generations reversed the extremes of the educational scale. Three fourths of the sons had gone to college or graduated, compared to slightly over one fourth of the fathers. In order to see how well educated the fathers were for their period, let us consider the figures for the total male population, fifty-five years and over, in 1940. Compared to fathers, twice as many men in the general population had less than high school education, and these comprised over three fourths of the group. Seven out of a 100 had gone to college or graduated, compared with 28 fathers—four times as many. The fathers of our 1952 business leaders, though far less educated than their sons, were far better educated than their contemporaries.

We have now only a general picture of the education of the two generations. More specifically, what was the education of the father of each son—whose sons went to college, whose did not? As we would expect, college-educated fathers had the largest proportion of college-educated sons, 91 per cent. But fathers with less than college education also had large percentages of college-educated sons: 80 per cent of the sons of men with high school education and 63 per cent of the sons of men with less than high school. The other groups follow the expected proportions, given the large percentage in each who went to college.

Although the education of the father is important in determining the education of the sons, it is far from the deciding factor. The proportions of college-educated sons decrease as the educational background of the father declines, but the fact that two thirds of the sons of men with less than high school would go to college shows that other factors are motivating these men, often against great financial odds and against the pattern of behavior of their group.

Combining the educational and occupational backgrounds of the fathers gives us a kind of picture of the environment in which the business leaders grew up and another measure of the cultural differences that existed among these men, in their formative years, who later came to share the business leadership of our country. Table III presents these figures and, in "Total for all leaders," indicates the proportions of business leaders coming from each educational background. Eighteen per cent of the business leaders are sons of college graduates, mostly professional and big business men; but more than twice as many are sons of men with less than

TABLE III.   OCCUPATION AND EDUCATION OF THE LEADER'S FATHER
(in percentages)

Occupation of Father	Education of Father					
	Less than High School	Some High School	High School Graduate	Some College	College Graduate	Total
Laborer—unskilled or semi-skilled	83	10	5	1	1	100
Laborer—skilled	67	18	11	3	1	100
Small owner	46	18	19	10	7	100
White collar	38	19	24	11	8	100
Major executive or large owner	22	15	26	14	23	100
Professional	6	5	7	13	69	100
Farmer	60	16	11	8	5	100
Total for all leaders	38	16	18	10	18	100

high school education, many of them skilled and unskilled laborers, farmers, small owners. Many of our present business leaders had a long way to travel to make good.

John B. Stone is one of these.[1] Now vice president of one of the world's largest producers of radio and television parts and high-fidelity sound equipment, Stone grew up in a small mill town in New England. His father, who had not even finished grammar school, worked as a common laborer in the mill. When the boy

[1] All quotations in this and the following chapters come directly from the business leaders or their wives; all descriptions of offices, homes, activities are taken from the field reports of the research staff. These were written at the time or immediately after the interview was given. Most leaders were interviewed at home and in their offices in order to get a larger perspective of the entire world of a man's career and to prepare the way for interviewing his wife. The only changes in the quotes or descriptions are those necessary to protect the anonymity of those interviewed.

For a full description of the methods used and a presentation of detailed statistical tables about the business leaders, see: Warner and Abegglen, op. cit. In our total study of the several thousand men or their wives, a significant number, selected as representatives of the various types, were interviewed.

was three years old, the father developed a heart ailment and was unable to work thereafter. When Stone was eighteen the father died. The illness of her husband put the support of the family and full responsibility for the children upon the mother, a strong woman of German descent, determined, hewing to the line and expecting her children to do the same.

"My mother was a marvelous person. She helped—encouraged me to get an education. I worked three years after graduating from high school and made $1880 and gave it to her so she could live while I went to college. I was the only one of the three children to go to college. My mother's sister criticized her for allowing me to go to school at all. You know, all the time I worked those three years I didn't spend any money at all, none at all; I gave it all to my mother.

"If it hadn't been for my mother I wouldn't have gone to college. I don't know, though. I associated in high school with a group of folks who had more money than I. I had certain talents which improved my lot to a certain extent. When we got out of high school I was the only one who didn't go on to college, but I was determined to go. So I set about working that out with my mother's help and encouragement. She didn't let me lose sight of that. I worked those three years after high school, and I worked all the time I went to college.

"Another reason I wanted to go to college was that I was determined to stay out of the paper mills. My father had worked there, my brother quit school at sixteen and got a job there, and I was determined to get out of that town and away from the mills. I had dreams of being a big executive, from the time I was a kid. I remember distinctly the big mill executives in town. I'd hear about them. That made a big impression on me.

"But when I was a kid I didn't do well in school. I wouldn't apply myself. I was thinking about other things. I would rather be outdoors. That was until I finished high school. I had poor grades in grammar school and high school, but in college I had excellent grades. I disliked chemistry, but I liked mathematics and

engineering and electricity. In college I was president of the fresh-
man class, vice president of the sophomore class, president of the
junior class, and in my senior year I was president of the student
council."

It was in high school that his mobility drives were clearly formed.
Attracted by the higher status of his friends, he wanted to go on to
college with them. His fear of having to work in the mills like his
father and brother and the encouragement of his mother aided
his ambition. With college Stone struck the pace that kept him
going on into a successful business career.

In the North, South, East, and West

Because of the differences among the regions of the United
States in the emphasis on education and in the kinds of education
offered, it seemed that there might be differences also in the education of business leaders according to where they were born and
grew up. Educational achievement was charted against four regions
of origin, and it was learned that little variation exists at any educational level among the regions: every region shows only a small
per cent with less than high school; they vary from 19 to 20 per
cent for high school; and from 76 to 77 per cent for college. When
the educational categories were redivided, the variations were still
small, the New England and Mountain states leading for college
graduates and postgraduates, the Southern states trailing, the
Middle Atlantic falling in between.

But when the educational achievement of the business leaders
is charted against the education of the general adult male population by region, we see a more complex picture. In the adult male
population the level of education is highest in the West, where 6
out of 10 men have attended high school or gone to college. The
North and Midwest are about equal; about half of the adult males
of these regions have more than grammar school education. The
general level of education is lowest in the South, where only 4 out
of 10 adult males have more than a grammar school education.
These differences in the educational level of the population, when

contrasted with the general similarities among business leaders, whatever their region of birth, point up one of the obstacles that must be overcome by men from the South in particular in moving into business leadership. Further, since on the whole an advanced education appears to be a prerequisite for most top business positions, these regional differences in education no doubt are an important cause of differing productivity of business leaders in the different geographic regions of the country.

Another aspect of education was examined for possible differences between American-born and foreign-born business leaders. The American-born category was divided into three: the leader American-born, but father foreign-born; the leader and father American-born; the leader, father, grandfather, and possibly other generations, American-born. The proportions who are college-educated are highest in this last category, decreasing regularly through the other two categories to "self foreign-born." The other levels of education, high school and less than high school, increase in proportions, in corresponding fashion. For the total group the business man who is foreign-born is least likely to have gone to college (6 out of 10), most likely to have stopped at grammar school (1 out of 10), and most likely to have gone only to high school (3 out of 10). At the other extreme are the figures for the business leaders whose grandfathers, at least, were American-born: 8 out of 10 have gone to college, less than 2 out of 10 (less than all other categories) have gone only to high school, and 2 out of 100 (less than all others) have less than high school education. When we compare the averages for each group with the overall averages for the entire group, we find that the leaders whose fathers were American-born have the same average educational achievement exactly as does the entire group of business leaders; that the leaders who are American-born, with foreign-born ancestors, and those who are foreign-born average less education; and those with longer ancestry here have more.

From another point of view, we are impressed by the fact that

6 out of every 10 business leaders who were foreign-born achieved a college education, and that 7 out of 10, of foreign-born parentage, were college men. The high old-American average, 8 out of 10, was only one and two points higher. The fact that people from other cultures can come to the United States and find higher education attainable and available as a possible route to business success indicates the degree of flexibility in our society in offering its resources to others and, in turn, having the advantage of their abilities and resources. In the same fashion, our society makes it possible for those most distant from the top to train themselves and ultimately achieve top positions; again, in making its resources available to these individuals, the society also gains. Moreover, for this situation to exist, not only must the resources of the society be made available, the individuals must be motivated to use them.

As we have seen earlier, one large and important segment of the business elite are "men in motion," who have come up the long distance from the bottom, and another segment, those energetic men who continue to be active at the same high occupational level as their fathers. Since territorial movement is associated with business success, we wanted to learn if education operated as a factor in the story of these "men in motion," whether those with higher education moved more often from their place of birth, how they moved, and where. Careful sampling has shown that, generally, the movements between states are longer and socially more important than those within a state. Therefore, we charted the movement in terms of whether the individual had stayed within his state or moved outside it.

Hypothetically it seemed that the college-educated man, mobile from the bottom, could move territorially to gain advantages since he would have the equipment to operate in more kinds of situations; that the mobile man with less education would tend to stay in a place with which he was familiar, where the variety of demands upon him would be more limited, where he would have more time to learn a job thoroughly.

In each group of the business elite, men who had less than college education tended to stay within their home states; those who had graduated from college went out of state in higher proportions. For both groups, movement anywhere was greater for the college graduates. When the origins of the business leaders are broken down into rural and urban, it is seen that education is a stronger factor than town or country in the amount of movement, although men of rural background, for all levels of education, are more likely to stay home.

Amount of education seems to take precedence over other variables—high or low status background, city or country—in determining the amount our business leaders have moved both within their home states and outside, sometimes to contiguous states, often to a state at some great distance. College tends to propel men over greater distances—it attracts and pulls them away from home and equips them to stay away if they find it to their advantage.

Education of Big Business Men Today and Yesterday

Business men today are much more highly educated than a generation ago. At the present time, almost 6 out of 10 of our business leaders have graduated from college and 2 more of the 10 have had some college training compared with about 3 out of 10 and a little over 1 out of 10 a generation ago (see Chart VI). Of course there has been an increase in level of education in the total population, but the increase among business leaders exceeds this greatly. In 1928, 32 per cent of the business leaders were college graduates; in 1952, 57 per cent.

The opinion is often expressed that the business career requires college preparation. In the month of January, 1954, more than six hundred large companies sent representatives to the nation's colleges in search of potential managerial talent. One reason for this was that the nation's big businesses have expanded more rapidly than their capacity to develop management material from within their ranks. The pressing need, moréover, is for "liberally schooled, broad-gauge executives—many-faceted men, for the highest posts." The search is among liberal arts graduates.

Irving Olds, retired board chairman of the U. S. Steel Corpora-

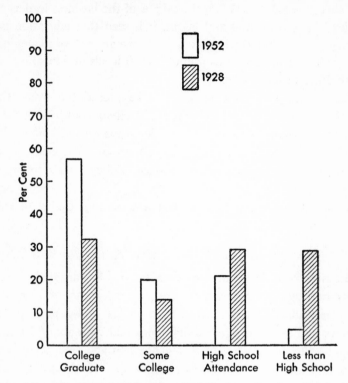

Chart VI.   How Much Education Did Business Leaders Get in 1928 and 1952?

tion, is quoted: "The most difficult problems American enterprise faces today are neither scientific nor technical but lie chiefly in the realm of what is embraced in a liberal arts education." And William G. Caples, vice president of Inland Steel: "Actually, the complexities of business are such that someone who understands history, literature, and philosophy, who is in a position to do some disciplined thinking, has the type of mind that will ultimately succeed [in business]."

At the same time, many businesses feel that they cannot afford the years of training of an executive and that they have the right to expect some specific, technical training in the young men they hire for potential management. Therefore, technical and business school training is also necessary.

The increased education we see among our present group of business leaders may be a point in a trend that will continue into the future. If this is so, it is important to see if there are significant differences between the 1928 and 1952 groups of business leaders in the amount of education according to their occupational backgrounds. Have some groups responded more than others to the demands for increased education; has it made much difference in the degrees of mobility?

The changes have been enormous. Smaller proportions of leaders from the lowest occupational backgrounds have less than high school education in 1952 than sons of large owners and executives a generation ago. In both periods farm and rural people tend to drop out of school earlier than urban people, but in the earlier generation the proportions were five times greater than they are today.

In 1952 the proportion of college graduates is almost twice as high as in 1928. In the earlier period, six occupational levels were below the average: skilled and unskilled workers, clerks, owners of small businesses, minor executives, and farmers. Today not only are all of these groups above their previous average, they are above the average for *all* of the elite a generation ago. Moreover, although these groups still fall below the general average for the current period, they more nearly approximate it than in the earlier period.

The educational achievement of both the mobile and birth elites has advanced markedly from 1928, those of lowest occupational background today having as high a proportion of college men as those of the highest-status background a generation ago. If this is a point in a trend, as it seems to be, then today's young men will have to be even more highly educated to become the business leaders of tomorrow.

What Colleges Educate Them?

Since the business elite are educated far beyond their contemporaries in the general population and far beyond the business leaders of a generation ago and since college graduates and postgraduates are distributed according to their occupational and geographic origins, it is important to learn about the kinds of colleges they went to. Did our 1952 business leaders attend some colleges more than others—Ivy League, state universities, or "cow colleges"? Were colleges offering technical training favored beyond those offering degrees in the liberal arts? Is there an apparent relation between the choice of college and the occupation and education of the father? For example, did those men born to the elite attend certain colleges more than others?

In this nation of ours, priding itself on its supposed high degree of literacy, are thousands of colleges representing a vast variety of sizes, purposes, faculties, and student bodies—and a corresponding variety of types and qualities of education. They range from the small sectarian institution and the small vocational college to enormous publicly supported agricultural and liberal arts universities, often with great graduate schools of specialized study in medicine, the law, business. To get at the important story of the *kinds* of colleges the business leaders attended, we selected a random sample of 505 college graduates from the group. We found that they had gone to a total of 194 different colleges and universities, both here and abroad, and that over one fourth of them had gone to more than one college, either as transfers during their undergraduate work or in seeking higher degrees.

Of the 505 business leaders in our sample, 216 went to only fourteen different colleges; and these same fourteen colleges were mentioned 87 times as the ones attended secondarily, either for graduate work or as a transfer college. Immediately we see a high concentration of attendance among a few most favored colleges:

	First or Only College Attended	Graduate or Second Undergraduate College Attended
Yale	36	9
Harvard	27	28
Princeton	20	1
Cornell	18	2
University of Pennsylvania	16	4
University of Illinois	13	3
Massachusetts Institute of Technology	13	6
University of Michigan	13	6
New York University	12	4
University of Minnesota	11	4
Williams College	10	—
University of California (Berkeley)	10	—
University of Chicago	9	7
Columbia University	8	13
Total	216	87

Almost one third of those listing one of these colleges first went to Harvard or Yale; exactly one third of both first and second mentions were these two colleges.

However, a sizable number went to a second select group of ten colleges. These colleges were mentioned first 62 times and second 17:

Northwestern University	7	7
Pennsylvania State	7	—
Stanford University	7	2
University of Wisconsin	7	2
Western Reserve University	7	1
Dartmouth	6	2
University of Washington	6	—
University of North Carolina	5	—
University of Pittsburgh	5	2
University of Texas	5	1
Total	62	17

Attendance for each of the other 194 colleges was a figure less than 5.

A glance at these lists shows that, in spite of the fact that a few are chosen far beyond all others, the favored colleges represent all regions of the country, state universities and those privately endowed, small colleges and large universities, technological institutions and those concentrating on the liberal arts. All are represented.

What kind of men selected what kind of college? What were the occupational backgrounds of those selecting some of the most favored colleges?

The large New England men's colleges, and Northwestern in the Middle West, and Stanford in the West, had the highest proportions of sons of major executives; almost one half of the business leaders going to these universities were of this occupational background. The small private Eastern colleges like Amherst and Colgate had the next highest proportion, over a fourth, and this figure was matched for sons of professional men bringing this group of colleges up to the big Eastern ones in their proportion of men of these combined backgrounds. Every college group represented had a fair proportion of sons of professional men except Northwestern and Stanford. The small proportion of professional representation in these universities is balanced by the comparatively large proportion of sons of white-collar workers, a proportion which is exceeded only at Pennsylvania University and Penn State. The lowest proportions of white-collar workers' sons were in the big New England universities and at Columbia and New York University.

Over three fourths of the future business leaders going to Harvard came from the larger business elite, including small owners, and only 12 per cent from the three most disadvantaged occupational groups. A sizable proportion too had grandfathers who were in the business elite: well over half were owners or executives or professional men, and almost one third were farmers.

Among all the large New England colleges, including Harvard,

Yale, Dartmouth, Princeton, and at Northwestern, and Stanford as well, there was not one son of a laborer. Not only were most of the fathers of Harvard men members of the professional and business elite, but over a third were college graduates. And yet over a half had only high school education or less: they represent a sizable group of successful men who had risen to the top in the previous generation without the benefit of college education. But it is a smaller group than the proportion of the fathers, of all the business leaders, who had a high school education or less; three fourths of the fathers had high school or less and only one fourth had gone to college or graduated.

All of the business leaders in our sample who went to Yale were the sons of business or professional men: over a third were the sons of major executives, a third the sons of professional men, and the remainder was divided between owners of large and small businesses. A very high proportion of the grandfathers, one in five, were professional men, and one half were of the top professional and business elite. None was a laborer. Over half of the fathers of Yale men were college educated, and the rest were about evenly divided between high school graduates and less.

Cornell University, fourth on the list for attendance, is the first one appearing on this attendance list to have laborers' sons from among our business leaders. Only a small per cent were sons of farmers, although Cornell has a large agricultural school as well as its liberal arts college and graduate schools. No sons of major executives in our selected sample went to Cornell; over a third were sons of professional men and over one fourth the sons of owners of small business. Farmers had the largest proportion among the grandfathers, over a third; a fourth were owners of small businesses; and one in five were professional men. There were no major executives or owners of large businesses among the grandfathers of Cornell men. A third of the fathers were college graduates and slightly more had less than a high school education.

The other colleges of the Ivy League follow the general attendance pattern of Harvard and Yale, with many fewer numbers of course, and each showing some special distinction. Princeton seems especially favored, although not so much as Yale, Williams, and Dartmouth are favored, by sons of major executives and professional men.

Columbia was selected especially by the sons of small owners. Being a large city university as well as an old established Ivy League college, Columbia presents a special picture in looking like New York University in some respects and in others like the colleges of the Ivy League.

We know from previous pages that slightly over half of the business leaders of laborer background either graduated from college or had some college education. But we have seen them represented here, when at all, only in the smallest proportions. Where do they go? What colleges are doing the job of educating these men—the important job that has helped them to realize their potential abilities and made it possible for our society to maintain, and even increase, the elasticity of status lines?

The large city universities, the state universities in the Big Ten, the Big Seven, and also in the South and West, and the specialized universities—M.I.T., Carnegie Tech., I.I.T.—and the very solid universities of Pennsylvania and Penn State educated more sons of laborers than the other colleges.

With the large proportion of business leaders graduating from the big Eastern colleges, one might expect a wide geographic representation among the group. Most of these colleges have attempted to spread their geographic and social base through a fortified scholarship program and a public-relations effort throughout the land. In the period when the business leaders in our study attended these colleges, this program was probably not yet launched; at any rate the geographic, as well as the social, base appears to be quite narrow as it is represented by our sample. Almost a third of the business leaders graduating from these favored colleges were from the Middle Atlantic states; over a fourth from New England; a fifth from the East North Central states; and a tenth from the West North Central.

Over a third of the business leaders who went to Harvard were from the New England states and about one in five from the Middle Atlantic and East North Central. Yale had the highest proportion from the Middle Atlantic. This is the area that sent its sons who were to become business leaders to college in many areas in high proportions: two thirds of the business leaders going to the small private Eastern colleges, to Cornell and Penn and Penn State, to Columbia and New York University, were from the Middle Atlantic states.

The small private Eastern colleges such as Haverford and Swarthmore, as well as Brown, Hamilton, etc., Cornell University, the University of Pennsylvania and Penn State all have large proportions from the Middle Atlantic states, and the technological universities approach the big Eastern colleges in leaders from this area.

Stanford and the Western state universities drew students from the Western area and, to some extent, from the South. The universities in the Big Ten and the Big Seven, Northwestern and Stanford, the state universities of the South—all drew heavily from their local areas.

The Kind of Education They Get

We studied the men in the college group to learn not only what institutions they attended but also what kind of education they selected. The 505 men earned 596 degrees, from every variety of institution of higher learning throughout the country. Of this total, over one third (211) were Bachelors of Art, a slightly higher proportion (232) Bachelors of Science, and 68 were specialized Bachelors degrees, primarily in preparation for business training (9 Bachelors of Business and 59 Bachelors of Law). Seventy-two received advanced degrees including Doctors of Philosophy and Science and Masters of Art. Thirteen of the total group were not classifiable. It is probable that many of the law degrees represent advanced training founded on the liberal arts.

Since such a high proportion of our present-day business leaders have graduated from college and even gone on to postgraduate work, it might be assumed that this would complete their formal education and that training for a career would then be undertaken entirely "on the job." But this is not so. From all occupational backgrounds, they continue to equip themselves through adult education with special knowledge necessary for their advancement. Comprehensive courses, business school training, commercial training within a college or university are all pursued. Most formal business training is in addition to the work done for college degrees.

Comparison with the leaders of a generation ago shows significant differences. Whereas 4 out of 10 present-day leaders report no extra business training, 7 out of 10 had no such training in the earlier period. Almost five times as many men have commercial training in a college or university today. In correspondence, public school, and business college courses, there is little difference between the two periods; the increase is in business courses in college or university and corresponds to the increase in college education in general. Those men below the college level are the ones who rely on correspondence and independent business school courses; the college men seek special training within the college.

Some differences exist between college and non-college men in taking more training; but an interesting fact is that college postgraduates and those with only grade school education are tied in taking extra work.

Men who have been ambitious to succeed apparently do not lose this ambition nor their ability to translate it into many forms of self-improvement that continue to enlarge their capacities and increase their skills and abilities. Since the demands made upon a top executive by a large organization are not confined within the company or even the industry but often are ramified by the community, the resources of the business leader may be great, but never enough. Fowler McCormick, board chairman of International Harvester, said in speaking of the training for business leadership: "It takes more than just business ability to make an

executive. Once a company reaches a certain size it becomes a
social institution with a definite responsibility. It cannot fulfill
this responsibility unless it is operated by a management educated
for this task."

Among the 1952 group of business leaders, how do the mobile
men compare with the birth elite in seeking increased training?
For the total group, an average of 58 per cent took special training
courses. The sons of laborers were above this average (7 out of 10)
and so were the sons of clerks, small owners, and farmers (6 out of
10); but the sons of major executives, large owners, and professional men were below (5 out of 10). It is the sons of lower
occupational levels who make this extra effort, yet about half of
the sons of big business and professional men also take specialized
training.

In comparing current figures with those of a generation ago, all
occupational backgrounds show great increases over the earlier
period in commercial training in colleges or universities. In training outside of college, changes are slight—in general the lower
occupational levels have increased while the higher ones have
remained about the same. The category of small business owner
offers a slight exception, dropping from 28 to 24 per cent between
the earlier and later periods. This corresponds to other evidence
that the owners of small business are increasingly following the
lead of big business men in sending their sons to college or using
college for special training to get ahead.

The measurable characteristic shared by our group of business
leaders to the highest degree is the amount of their education.
They have become, to a large extent, a professional class which
demands formal training and preparation, over a broad field of
knowledge as well as in technical areas, as prerequisites to a successful career. Education has become the royal road to positions
of power and prestige in American business and industry. That
this royal road is open to all men is given ample testimony by
the large number of educated men from the bottom social layers
who appear in our sample.

A large proportion of these successful business men went to a small number of colleges which have gained the reputation of giving the best training for successful careers in the business world. This concentration has been augmented by the fact that they are considered the best recruiting grounds for future leaders by Big Business. Yet some of the giants, the mail order houses, prefer to recruit their potential leaders from state universities where they find men who have not lost touch with the vast masses of people whose hopes and desires create the greatest market of all.

Yet, despite the concentration among a few favored colleges and universities, every kind of college was represented in our sample and for a variety of reasons. Some colleges were chosen because "my father went there" or "the men in my family have always gone there." Others were chosen because, financially, they were the only ones available—denominational schools with liberal scholarships and low tuition and living costs, state universities, especially if nearby, the college in the home town. Some leaders who showed signs of successful endeavor in high school received scholarships. Increasingly our large private universities and technical schools are adopting a policy of higher tuition costs that will permit an enlarged scholarship program. They state this explicitly. They want to insure that they will maintain their competitive position in attracting the best scholars. This means, of course, that the middle-grade students who attend these universities, and their families, are in fact subsidizing the education of those of more ability or financial need. It has other implications: increasingly competitive scholastic competition within the university is one. Another is that the society as a whole should ultimately profit from having its people of highest ability, regardless of social or economic background, given the best possible training—and in educational institutions where they will be noticed by the business institutions who need them and where they will have the best opportunity for a successful career. The successful career of an individual implies profit of various sorts not only for him but for the organization which he serves and for the society of which it is a segment.

4

The Private Worlds
of Mobile Men

Transition: Going To Is Away From

Although American business leadership is made up of men of many backgrounds who differ in numerous and varied ways, we find them in their maturity at a common point, a position in which they wield far-reaching and formidable business power. They have made their way to this position through a variety of channels and methods.

In general, these men have assigned themselves (or our society has assigned to them) tasks that have many elements in common. Each has been required to move through a succession of jobs, presenting problems of learning, acquiring skills, establishing relationships, successful accomplishment. This job movement has culminated for every man in a position of major executive authority and responsibility in a central and dominant business concern.

As part of this movement to higher business positions, and in order to establish his position securely in the business elite, the successful man has had to undertake a series of social movements. He has progressed from the young school boy, involved with and dependent upon his family, through the life stages, to the establishment of his own family as an integrated group in the community. He has moved in friendship patterns from youthful cliques and gangs to powerful and prestigeful clubs and social groups in the large American cities.

Broadly, then, each of the members of the business elite confronts in the course of his life career this dual task. He must achieve and maintain his occupational position as an executive in the business hierarchy, and he must establish himself and his family as accepted and respected members of the social hierarchy of his community.

These two tasks are interdependent and occur as interwoven and interacting themes in the life of the business man. His job succession provides him the income and some of the prestige on which his community position depends. In no small measure his community position advances or impedes his progress in the business hierarchy.

Let us state a few major generalizations about the careers of the business elite. By this we will establish some of the basic conditions within which the different personalities function, and we will refresh ourselves about the findings given in earlier chapters. Furthermore, by so doing, we can bring the problem into sharper focus.

In the upper level of business the many varieties of men, in terms of differences in backgrounds, careers, skills, and personalities, have found many ways to work through their career problems. A study of men at two extremes was undertaken with the expectation that the contrasts would reveal the working of the total mobility forces more pointedly. These are the men who differ most from each other in the social and occupational position from which they began their careers. The first is the mobile group, men whose fathers were laborers and clerks, and who have traversed the maximum social distance to reach the top. The second group, the birth elite, are those men whose fathers were business leaders and who hold their positions in the same firm as their fathers.

The story of the mobile group is the fulfillment of the American Dream. These are the men who have come the long way from birth into a family in meager circumstances, with little social prestige and less economic power. They are the men with little formal education and long hours of night school, those who worked their way through college, who learned as they moved. They are the *nouveau* and, if not rich, much more affluent than an observer at their birth would have predicted. Shouldering out of their way the many competitors passed en route, they are the reaffirmation of our society's great myth—log cabin to the White House, Steeltown to Park Avenue, tailor shop to Carnegie Hall.

The birth elite are at the other extreme, for they are the inheritors who retain the positions their fathers held before them. Their number is no smaller than the mobile men among business leaders. Their careers do not fit the ever-fascinating drama of hard-won success Americans stage for themselves. Indeed their lives, by virtue of the seeming ease of succession to high position, are in one sense a denial of the American Dream, and often are uncomfortably felt to be a refutation of our principles of equal opportunity. The backgrounds of these men make their careers seem less trying, less difficult, than the career task of the mobile man; their success seems less ennobling, no more than might be expected, for "they had all the advantages."

But the birth elite are also confronted with the task of job movement. They too must successfully prove themselves and must move from one job to another before succeeding to their father's position. This is made more difficult by the shadow of a powerful father, whose looming figure may well prevent the son from becoming the man he must be for ultimate succession to his father's position. Moreover, the men in the birth elite must overcome the repugnance commonly felt in our community and business life toward this kind of career.

Thus, when looking at occupational mobility, we must keep in mind two different types of movement. The first is from a lower-level occupational background to a position in the business elite—movement out of the occupation of the father, through a succession of job positions, to an elite position, at a new and distant social level. The second is movement from an elite background to an elite position: the men in the birth elite must move through a series of occupations and establish in their own persons the status their fathers occupied, at the same social level.

The mobile men have moved over the longest social distances. They are identified by the fact that their present position in terms of prestige and income is far removed from the occupation of their fathers—the occupation into which they were born. But the movement of these men is not merely nor even primarily occupational. The positions they now hold are simply a measure and single example of a continual, never-ending process of social movement that characterizes every phase of their lives.

The mobility here is a total process. Before all, these are men on the move. They left their homes, and all that this implies. They have left behind a standard of living, level of income, and style of life to adopt a way of living entirely different from that into which they were born. The mobile man first of all leaves the physical setting of his birth. This includes the house he lived in, the neighborhood he knew, and in many cases even the city, state, and region in which he was born.

This physical departure is only a small part of the total process of leaving that the mobile man must undergo. He must leave behind people as well as places. The friends of earlier years must be left, for acquaintances of the lower-status past are incompatible with the successful present. Often the church of his birth is left, along with the clubs and cliques of his family and of his youth. But most important of all, and this is the great problem of the man on the move, he must to some degree leave his father, mother, brothers, and sisters, along with the other human relationships of his past.

In addition to these great and expensive departures, the mobile man must leave behind the ways of behaving, the sets of manners, and the attitudes toward other people of his early training. He must search out, learn, and employ new ways, manners, and attitudes appropriate to his new position. These extend from such relatively simple matters as taste in clothing to the complexities of speech, of eating and drinking.

Social mobility is a continuous process. The mobile man finds an occupation different from that of his father. This is only the first of a long series of moves, from occupation to occupation, position to position. For most of these men, this movement is endless, the endpoint always receding beyond the attained or immediately attainable. There is always a further step in the series. Each arrival dictates a departure, as the man drives himself further along his course.

As in the occupational moves, so with the other departures the mobile man makes. He leaves his earlier circumstances for a different life style, as he moves from position to position. Each job change means leaving a set of friends, meeting new persons, becoming involved with them, and in turn leaving that group for yet another with another job move. Friends appropriate to a skilled laborer have somehow less in common with a foreman, and the foreman's friends little chance to get together with the plant superintendent, while the superintendent's friends live in a different neighborhood from that into which the vice president has moved. The three-room apartment is left behind for a duplex, after which the children need to be taken to a suburb for the schools (or because the place we have is too small or because everyone we know lives in Forestdale). Each of these changes of house and neighborhood brings with it myriad changes large and small, from home furnishings to clubs, to vacation habits, to the children's schools.

Mobility may be seen as a continual process of departing-arriving-departing, and . . . The mobile man is that person who is able successfully to initiate and sustain this complex, interwoven series of changes. He must learn, rapidly and thoroughly, the new behaviors in each new situation. He must be able to tolerate uprooting himself and to make use of, or create, the opportunities to move to a new position. He must be able to leave his past behind as he moves into each new present.

In the limited space available we cannot present all our findings about the variety of personalities among the mobile men and those in the birth elite. We will first concentrate our attention on Donald Hayes and devote sufficient time to him to bring out some of the salient characteristics of an important type of mobile man. Later in this chapter we shall briefly refer to others to indicate some of the variations in personality and in Chapter VIII we shall examine the personalities of representative men from the birth elite.

The Personality of Donald Hayes: One Type of Successful Man

Like most of the mobile men interviewed, Donald Hayes gave few details concerning the kind of life he lived as a boy. That it was not an easy or affluent one is clear enough. His father was a machinist and the family lived in Cleveland. "My father used to like to drink, and spent little time at home. I can't remember my father ever doing anything for us. Yes, my mother had to work. She took in washing, and we were still delivering it until after we were married. Mother was always even-tempered, hard-working. She made a good home with what she had to do with. She was always serious but she was a good mother. She had to make all our clothes and there were five boys to take care of."

Mr. Hayes' parents disagreed about money often. "We were afraid of my father, and so was my mother. I never saw my father comb his hair or tie his shoelaces; my mother did it for him. Of course we didn't see my father much as he just wasn't around."

Asked further for childhood memories, Hayes said: "It was just hard work! Period. It was hard work on my wife's side too. That's why we appreciate the dollar today." A little more information about the financial circumstances of Mr. Hayes' childhood came out when in speaking of his fondness for school he also remarked, "I used to sweep the school at three cents a room." An early and acute consciousness of differences between himself and others existed—"A kid I knew had the most of any of the fellows I played with. His father had a good position. He got a new suit all the time. That's what I used to admire him for."

Hayes was born the son of an occasionally employed laborer, primarily supported by his mother's work as a laundress. He does not suggest that he was acutely deprived as a child but, rather, that the family lived in constant financial difficulty.

Some notion of the distance this man has come may be gathered from the interviewer's description of the home he now lives in. "Mr. Hayes said, 'We don't have any [numbered] address, but the house is located on Ocean Avenue, the second house east of Washington Road.' I had no difficulty finding it from this description and was interested to see, as I neared the place, that the area is just recently developed. All the residences seem fairly new, and very substantial, though not in the estate class. Most of the houses are set well back from the road and have numerous old trees around them. There is considerable acreage still in woods. The Hayeses had lived in this house only five weeks when I arrived. It is a stone ranch house of good but not distinctive design or proportions. The lawn is already thick with grass, and there are three acres of it. 'You have to have at least three acres to build out here.'

"When I arrived the Hayeses were sitting on a rear terrace talking. Although it is not screened and the mosquitoes were rather a bother, we continued sitting there until it was quite dark. 'Let us show you the house,' Mr. Hayes said as we went in. 'After all, we're rather proud of it.' The house is equipped with all the latest in streamlined kitchens and dressing rooms, sliding doors, and the rest. Each of the three bedrooms had its gay, streamlined bath. The furniture was purchased new for the house and is of rich woods and fabrics, but the total effect in each room is lacking in charm and sometimes in harmony. Under a large picture window in the living room there is a stiff, curved davenport covered in a metallic upholstery. I remarked about the attractive stone fireplace, and Mrs. Hayes said, 'We probably won't use it much; we're afraid of getting the ceiling dirty.' We sat widely separated in three corners of the room, because of the arrangement of the furniture."

The stiff, new surroundings in which we find Donald Hayes provide a measure of the distance he has traveled in becoming executive vice president of Allied Products, Inc., a manufacturing firm of central importance in its field. On the pine-paneled walls of his office are pictures of the chairman of the board of his company and executives of other manufacturing firms. "They're all friends."

Hayes is, on the whole, typical of mobile men in American business. His father was more unpleasant than many; his present circumstances a little less comfortably fitting than some. Still he represents a type, and a look at the road he has traveled and the manner in which he moved over it will aid in understanding what kinds of men these mobile men are, and how they happened to take this road.

"My first job was when I was twelve, pulling weeds in a factory farm. During the first three years of high school I worked after school and in the summers at a store in town. McLean, the owner, was a Scotchman and typical of the race. He couldn't tolerate idleness or waste. I had to mop up the floors and then go through the accumulated waste for pins. Mr. McLean made a lasting impression on me.

"I liked school a lot. Did well in it. I finished high school in mid-year and had an idea that I would like to go on to college. I looked around for a temporary job, and got one with a floating repair gang on the railroad. I found out that I wouldn't have enough left to pay for college, and I didn't like the repair gang work, so I left after a couple of months and got a job with an advertising agent in Seattle. I liked to travel a lot—I guess all kids that age do. So I went back to the railroad in their freight office in San Francisco. But the idea of college and more education kept gnawing at me so I left the railroad and enrolled in Ohio College, in the law school. I wasn't interested in becoming a lawyer but I thought I could get some business law which would help me. After a year I ran out of money and the only thing to do was to go back to business. In 1920 I got a job in a machine shop—it required no training and the boom was still on and I got $75 to $80 per week."

Hayes stayed on this last job only a half year because "the bottom dropped out of the boom and the department was laid off." He found machine work of various kinds after that, but "knew the bitterness of unemployment." He tried selling door to door and shop to shop. During this period he started haunting the public library, reading "everything I could get on corporation finance.

There was no pattern to my reading; I just definitely did not want to do laborer or machine shop work forever. But I had begun to get crazy about production and heavy industry. I finally got a job at Universal Steel in their plant." Hayes said that in five months he was offered the job of assistant foreman. When I asked if he was surprised by the rapid promotion, he replied, "No, I expected it. I still want and expect better things."

In 1934, Hayes said, he got "ambitious." "Three of us with the company decided to start our own fabricating plant in Detroit. This was the Midwest Pipe and Wire Company. One of the others was president, I was vice president, and the third man was secretary. They were not active though. One was too old and the other had too much money. We hardly made out for the first few years and then received federal war contracts in 1941 which really boomed the business. By 1948 I was made chairman of the board and when the company was bought out by Allied Products I was made a director and vice president of the company."

This kind of movement through a succession of jobs culminating in his present position of prestige and authority is not random nor chance movement. The theme of training, formal and informal, runs through the rapid succession of job changes in earlier years. It must be imagined, for Hayes is not explicit about it, that he learned in each situation not only skills and techniques in production and corporation problems but additional social skills. In each new situation he was able to capitalize further on his new learning. After this long apprenticeship he was able to seek out, and become attached to, a few men with whom and through whom he moved into a position with real status potential.

Each of these seemingly random moves meant a change in type of work, in friends, and in location. Each represents a departure and each new situation an arrival at a way-station en route to subsequent departure. Nowhere in this review of his career does Hayes mention his family. There is no indication that he was in touch with his parents or brothers and sisters, nor even that they were a consideration in his moves.

Asked about his activities outside of the business world, he replied, "I'm very much interested in health. I'm president of the Memorial Hospital in Forestdale, and a director of the Stevens Hospital in the city. Then I'm a member of the Athletic Club and the Union League Club. We belong to the Forestdale Country Club and have for some time. I'm a past president of the Association of Commerce and Industry and a member of the Industrial Employers Board. Also the National Association of Manufacturers."

We have a picture of a mobile man, a man from a poor and difficult background, who has worked his way through a variety of situations and locations to arrive at some eminence as a business and community leader. We find him at fifty-five years of age on a kind of plateau, with a new home, relatively new business position, solid community position, and able to review his career and life with some satisfaction.

Against this outline of the basic events in the social mobility of Donald Hayes it is now possible to ask what kind of person he is. What set off all this movement? What is a man like who accomplishes all this? How does he approach the world and how does he feel about other people? The interview with him provides a good deal of information, and the analysis of the Thematic Apperception Test[1] material provides more.

First, it is clear that a man like this must be intelligent. The amount and variety of learning that have taken place and must take place for mobility to occur indicate at least an average, and probably higher, intellect mastering the many tasks involved. However, Hayes is not outstandingly bright. His ability to learn rapidly

[1] The Thematic Apperception Test was invented by Professor Henry Murray, of Harvard University (see *Explorations in Personality*, Oxford University Press, 1938). It provides evidence and understanding about the organization of the psychic life of the individual, probing beneath the conscious level to the deeper emotional structure of the personality. Such people as Harriet Moore, of Social Research, Inc. of Chicago, and Professor William Henry, of the University of Chicago, have adapted it for the practical purposes of business administration. Many business firms now use this instrument for the evaluation and selection of personnel.

and to adjust effectively to new situations depends on additional qualities. From the TAT:

Hayes is a bright man, of above average intelligence, without any great brilliance or creativity. He is not a highly imaginative person, but rather works within the facts and situation at hand. He is direct in his approach to problems, and does not get involved in either details of situations or in side-issues. He organizes his thinking well, and is markedly crisp and decisive, making up his mind quickly and following his line of thought through to a solid and definite conclusion. He does not look for problems in his approach to situations, but takes them as he finds them. Further, he does not appear much aware of an audience as he works. Rather, he works for the personal satisfactions it brings him—because he must, in other words, because he is that kind of person. He is not at all a show-off and is notably realistic and accurate in his judgments.

For the process of mobility, certain of these facts about Hayes' approach to his world seem critical. His thinking is realistic and direct, and he has the ability to size up problems without becoming emotionally involved in them. Still more important in the light of his career is the fact that, in his approach to situations, he is firmly oriented to getting the task at hand accomplished. He keeps a tight rein on his abilities and energies and directs them, without distraction, to the goals he has set himself. A substantial level of intelligence is necessary, but these other qualities are undoubtedly important in terms of his achievement.

Furthermore, this is an energetic man. Throughout his career he has been able to pour a tremendous amount of energy into meeting the tasks ahead; he does not dissipate his energy over a wide range of activities but concentrates to a maximum degree on the total career process. As with intelligence, this energy matter in mobile men is not simply a matter of level of energy. More important is that they are able, to a singular degree, to devote all their available energies to the solution of immediate and practical goals. They do not think of, or allow themselves, the luxury of a range of interests or activities. The effects of this are felt by their wives, their children, their friends, and their society.

But, granted that these men are tough-minded, bright, and energetic realists, what is their approach to their world? How do they act toward other people, toward their family and friends, and how do they see themselves as persons? The central thread running through the web of Hayes' social relations is his experiences in, and feelings about, his family. Hayes indicates at several points in the interview that his parents' relationship with their families was a strained one. "There were always clashes between my father's side of the family and my mother's side because her people were very good Catholics, and we were never considered part of the family because we weren't Catholics." Apart from this religious difference, "they were hard workers on my mother's side, but not on my father's. They were German on both sides. I never associated with my father's mother or father. I can remember my mother's father playing with me, but I cannot remember his ever coming into the house. I don't know why." Hayes' earliest memory is the consciousness of a split between the parental and grandparental generations, both in terms of religion and in terms, presumably, of a rejection by his mother's family of the man she married.

That Hayes, too, felt his father inadequate is clear. While he describes his mother as even-tempered, hard-working, and a good homemaker, he says of his father: "He was very hot-tempered. He was hard on all his boys as long as he was able to swing a stick. . . . As for childhood worries, I worried about my father's condition, and that he might hurt my mother." Of his mother and father he said, "My mother was very good at getting along with people. Maybe I learned a little of that from her. About the only thing I can remember my father saying is, 'Go to work.' "

This picture of the parents and Hayes' feelings about them is amplified through the TAT.

Hayes portrays his home as an emotionally and physically impoverished place, and the people in it as being in conflict with each other. His description of the mother is of a stern, rigid, moral person. She appears to him to be a person who tries to control him and to be repressive rather than giving him the independence he demands. He appears to be concerned over the fact that he found it necessary to reject the advice, rules, and guidance his mother pressed on him, but he feels a deep need to be a self-directing person and moved gently but firmly away from her control.

At the same time, it is clear that he felt his mother cared for him and was aware of her interest and concern over him. He portrays his mother as attempting to negotiate and smooth over differences between his father and himself, and it is his mother who wants him to remain in the home in the face of the indifference and outright rejection of him by his father.

The directness with which some of these underlying feelings were expressed and the sharpness with which they are felt by Hayes are indicated by this explicit response to a TAT picture showing a young man and an older woman alone in a room, the woman with her back turned to the man.

This young fellow, I think, has had a spat or fight with his father. His father's told him to get out and the mother's tried to act as a peacemaker and she's failed. She wanted the boy to stay and I think he's going to leave anyway. The mother doesn't want to see him go. [What was the fight about?] Money. The boy got in some kind of trouble and he tried to get his father to bail him out, and his father said no.

Here in this single story is the family conflict, the assistance and support given by the mother, and the need for the boy to leave the home. There is, it should be noted, no real regret over leaving indicated. The father and the boy have been fighting, the father has rejected the boy, and this precipitates the departure. The reason for the fight between father and son is the failure or refusal of the father to come to the boy's aid against the authorities and, more especially, to be unable or unwilling to help the boy financially. Here we see both the emotional and economic deprivation touched on in the context of the family.

The TAT analysis goes further into Hayes' feelings about his father:

He indicates that his father was indifferent to him, and simply did not care for him or about him. Further the father is shown to be actually rejecting him. However, through all of this there are indications that the father is a basically attractive and positive figure for Hayes. He very much wanted his father to be trustworthy, to be helpful, to be more interested in him, and to be a source of advice, aid, and affection. In this he was not, it would appear, totally disappointed, but rather the father was inconsistent and generally indifferent or rejecting. In his whole approach to his family experiences, Hayes perhaps sums it up in the line he uses in one story, "This fellow appears to be escaping from something."

It may be possible at this point to put some of these elements together in trying to get at the style of this man. He is the son of a woman who was moralistic, and controlling, who presumably trained him to be reserved, to obey the rules of his society, to be proper, respectable, and hard-working. Further, since her background seems to have been superior to her present circumstance, it seems likely that she was able to begin the training for a different social world as well as provide both an example and glimpses of it.

Hayes is the son of an unreliable, apparently rather dangerous, certainly unsatisfying father. Neither from mother nor father did he get the kind of emotional satisfactions that might make him an easy or comfortable person. On the contrary, he learned that his home was inadequate and that he must "escape" it to achieve the goals his mother perhaps, among others, helped set for him. From this background Hayes emerged an independent and solitary figure. Again from the TAT we find that:

He is first of all a man who must set his own goals and tasks. He sees himself as an independent person, although on the whole he does not introspect about himself or his behavior. His relations with authority, sharply affected by his basic experience with his father, will be cautious and reserved. He waits upon proof that he can trust others, and is most reluctant to put himself in a position of dependence on others. Doubtless this is a result of his family experiences of unreliability.

To restate this, Hayes is a man who is involved in repeatedly demonstrating to himself and to others that he does not need them, that he is able to conduct his own life successfully through his own abilities.

The result is a single-purposed, tense individual who can never rest. He tells the interviewer, "I've always been interested in production. I like something moving, and always wanted to have a lot of men working for me. I'm interested in anything that produces fast. If I could ever get the job done, with everything perfect, then I'd be ready for something else. But there's always expansion, then you have to digest that and make it run like a well-oiled machine."

The intensity and sharp focus of drive in this man have left little interest, time, or energy for anything outside his career. He first of all does not find it easy to get along with other men. His attitude toward them, perhaps basically a result of his relations with his father, seems mixed. The TAT analysis states:

Hayes' relations with other men are marked by two definite and seemingly incompatible reactions. He is not himself an outgoing hail-fellow type, but waits to be approached generally. He is, however, very positive in his feeling toward other men. He likes to feel that they are interested in him, and he gets great satisfaction from being with them. However, and this counter-current runs strong, Hayes does not really trust other men, for he believes that if he places reliance on them, they will or at least are likely to let him down. He will therefore by choice make some effort to work with other men in a solid and cooperative manner. He does not really feel competitive toward them and is quite willing to share his work where possible. At the same time he does not believe basically that this cooperative arrangement will work out, for he sees other men as unreliable. Therefore he believes he must fall back on his own resources and make his own way unaided.

Interesting confirmation of this view that Hayes is on the whole unable or unwilling to be involved with other people comes from the interview, in discussing the social activities of the Hayeses. "Well, our friends are my wife's sister and her husband. We don't have a large circle of friends, and they are pretty scattered. Old friends from school, say, are dead, or in Cleveland, or scattered.

I don't have time to see my old friends when I'm there. You know, when a fellow succeeds, a lot of people envy him. We just lead an ordinary life. You saw us sitting on the terrace when you drove up. That's the kind of people we are. I don't believe in having close friends in the company either, 'cause generally those things backfire. Neither of us sees much of the business associates socially." Mrs. Hayes added, "I'm just an old-fashioned mother. I don't belong to any women's clubs. My family keeps me busy." (Both offspring are adults.)

This relative isolation on the part of an apparent leader in his community is no doubt a result of several, perhaps inevitable, aspects of the life of the mobile man in America. There is a note of apology and defensiveness in these remarks about a limited number of friends. But it is hard to see how a man like this, utterly concentrating on his job and career, moving rapidly and far, cut off by need and intent from his past, could retain friends or acquaintances. Add to all this the fact that an essential part of his approach to his life is a need to work alone, and a mistrust of others, and the result is isolation. Where this is the case the career of the mobile man carries the seeds of its own destruction. The isolation is, on the whole, necessary to the kind of mobility he has experienced. Yet to be really mobile, and to achieve a solid status at the top level of the community, he must be able to interact with people easily and to become a part not just of the business world but of the wider social community.

Like all of these mobile men, Hayes is married—like most, he married when he was rather young. Like his other relationships, his marriage is another measure of the kind of relations with people and approach to life that he has developed. The TAT analysis says this:

In a total picture of limited and cautious relations with others and of controlled emotions, Hayes' relations with women are undoubtedly most limited. He could by no means be called a sensual man. Sexuality appears to play little part in his behavior directly. He portrays relations with women as essentially distracting and frivolous. Although there is no indication that he feels himself to be sexually inadequate, and such a problem would be inconsistent with his generally high level of self-confidence, he does portray women as sexual aggressors and himself as determined not to get involved with them as sexual objects. He appears to divorce his home and wife from sexuality and rather portrays his relations in the home as comfortable, and essentially asexual.

Some confirmation of Hayes' attitude toward his home as a protected haven is provided in the interview where he remarks of his wife's social activity: "Mrs. Hayes doesn't have time for after-noon bridge parties or cocktail parties; we don't go to night clubs. Certain things creep into a man's life that way, and you begin to worry about what each other is doing. You can't work that way. It usually ends in a broken home. I don't think you can burn the candle at both ends. We'll build another house; that will keep us busy." Again we find the concentration and the need for independence which is seen as a minimum involvement with other people.

Their Parents and Early Experiences

The personality and career pattern of Donald Hayes are, on the whole, representative of the majority of the mobile men studied. In light of this single case, and looking at the entire group and at the process of social mobility, what can we say of the nature of socially mobile men?

It is clear that these men are both willing and able to initiate and sustain the process of departure, arrival, and departure necessary to social mobility. Departure, emotionally and physically, from the home is a task assigned all men in our culture. Not all accomplish this task, but maturity as we see it depends among other matters on the ability to break the ties to the parents to a degree sufficient to enable the maturing child to function as a social entity separate from his family of birth. It is incumbent on the adult male in our society to establish his own home, and, in full social develop-ment, to establish his own family, and raise his children.

Because he learns to be a social person through his family of birth, a man will often establish a home that resembles in furnishings and atmosphere his own home. He will often reproduce in his career much of the social position, attitudes, and behaviors of his own family. Most men follow closely, if not exactly, the occupations of their fathers, and on the whole occupy a similar position in the community.

If all of this is less true of American men than of the men of other countries, we may no doubt attribute this difference to the much greater amount of social mobility of all kinds that takes place between generations of Americans. For it is the first requisite of the mobile man that he leave his home, and that the break from his parents and their entire way of life be rapid and marked.

Donald Hayes made this break. He is "escaping from something," from the impoverishment of his home, first of all, from the spiritually bleak and physically depressed family atmosphere. The inheritance of Donald Hayes from his father was an intangible but rewarding one from the mobility standpoint, as it turned out, for he learned through his relations with his father not to be or become like him. He learned from his mother the kind of approach to the world and its tasks that made it possible for him to be a productive and energetic person, working within the moral rules of our society to get the rewards that he had been trained to expect.

This set of attitudes toward the home and parents is not true of Hayes alone. The remarks of some of the other mobile men interviewed concerning their parents may serve to make this area more clear.

Mr. R.: "My father was a plumber, and he was an invalid for I'd say the last twenty years of his life. My father was not a happy person when I knew him. I never knew him when he wasn't an invalid. He had arthritis. They called it something else then. He had terrible spells. Apparently he had a good disposition early in life. My father and mother didn't get along well. His terrible disposition was caused, I guess, to some extent by his pain and incapacity." [Later, of his mother] "My mother was a very determined person, strictly disciplined. She was a person of the old school who believed in bringing up her children along a straight line. She had all the responsibility of bringing up the kids. My mother was very religious; she was a marvelous person; she helped—encouraged me to get an education. Her sister criticized her for letting me go to school. But I wasn't close to my mother or my father. She was too strict; too much discipline. She beat the hell out of you as a kid. When I was older, she yelled. I resented it. Probably did me good though."

Mr. Y.: "They had arguments. That's about all that I remember. It seems to me that I had an idea that I didn't like the atmosphere. As a kid I had the idea of getting out, of getting away from the steel mill."

Mr. D.: [What kind of man was your father?] "He was easygoing in one way. He had a wonderful sense of humor although he was very strict. A lot of German in him. My parents were divorced when I was about sixteen. I never did get along with him. He was too strict and stubborn. I just couldn't see eye to eye with him. I didn't have much to do with him when he was at home. I avoided him most of the time." [Of his mother] "My mother was a dynamic woman. Full of pep and never satisfied. She had plenty of drive. I always went to her for advice, and she wanted me to get ahead. She was always in favor of my doing whatever would help me to get ahead. I generally took advice from my mother. I avoided my father as much as possible."

Mr. K.: "I had a very religious father, ultra-religious. I couldn't quite agree with him about religion but he thought he was right. My father was a strait-laced disciplinarian. We toed the mark if you get the point. My mother just lived for her family, no sacrifice was too great. She sacrificed herself for her children. The odd part of it was that for many years she never went out, until after my father's death. Yet after his death she belonged to everything, all kinds of groups and clubs. My mother gave me the impetus; she was quite a pusher."

Generally the focus of energy on mobility derives from the mothers. At the same time, the TAT indicates some negative feeling toward the mother as the figure who attempts to hold and control the son. The fathers seem in most cases to have been distant from the sons, and not at all supporting or reinforcing. The father is an unreliable figure. At the same time, there is this feeling of loss and deprivation, that the father is withholding something from the son that he might provide, and some of the process of mobility may be seen as an effort to gain this withheld support, and to prove oneself a worthy and able figure in the eyes of the father.

This complex of attitudes appears to form the basis for the initial departure of the mobile man—a real emotional departure from the parental figures at the personality level. This basic separation from the family will be much less likely to occur among individuals whose antecedents have for generations been identified with a single community, or sometimes a single house or farm, and where there are extensive and close ties with many people in the community. Without exception, the mobile men in our study describe their families as not involved in community activities, and there appear to be but few instances where any substantial inter-action took place with the wider circle of blood relations. In the case of Donald Hayes, his own family was cut off from the wider kinship group of grandparents.

A problem in understanding many of the mobile men involves the fact that a troubled or unsatisfactory home, such as they describe, is held to be a fundamental factor in the widest range of special groups, and especially to be a factor in maladjustment and behavior disorders. What then makes it possible for these men to make the kind of social adjustment they do—almost to exploit to their advantage a situation that wrecks the lives of others? Certainly the nature of the mother is important, for apparently it is through her that these men learn to strive, to work hard today for rewards that may possibly be forthcoming at some future time, and deeply believe in this. Also, and unlike the typical history of social maladjustment, these men seem to have during their adolescent years positive experiences with male figures, and to have experiences that reinforce the training and life-view implanted by the mother.

Hayes did not provide substantial information in this area, but other cases do. One mobile man commented, "I always had a lot of friends [as a child], more than I have now as an adult. Always participated actively in athletics with success. We lived in a modest neighborhood a little beyond our means because the folks wanted it for us kids. I ran with kids not so different from myself. We didn't have much to do with the kids over on the hill or they with us. Yes, we had gangs always, though mostly they were for football or baseball. I was always leader of the gang." His wife interjected, "His mother says Bill was always president of everything he ever joined." "When we moved to Springfield I went to a high school where the wealthy kids went, and there were a lot of differences. I'd be lying if I said I wasn't bothered because of the differences—in clothes, and the places we went and lived in. These things worried me."

Repeatedly in the interviews there were passing references to success in athletics, or in music, or to recognition through offices and honors. Usually these men lay no claim to academic honors in their youth, nor would the level of intelligence of most indicate conspicuous scholarly success. But by virtue of skills, chance, or perseverance, they have been able to experience in some meaningful measure the rewards promised by their early training. They have found, and doubtless to be mobile must find, that by driving for a goal they will be able to reach it or come very close.

Another element of central importance is the experience of some father-figure who gave them encouragement and aid, and thereby ameliorated their hostility toward males by fulfilling some of the functions they feel their fathers have neglected. These men seem most often to have been teachers. For example, Hayes said, "The principal of the junior high school was a driver. He could get people to do things no one else could get them to do. Perhaps I learned a little from him." Another such figure often cited is the athletic coach. This fact is particularly important when it is noted that in most types of American careers, including business careers, the sponsor-protégé relationship is an important element in the total training process. The ability to attract the attention of these older and more highly placed men and to learn rapidly from them is of considerable advantage. Denied satisfying relationships with the father, these mobile men are well equipped psychologically to accept relationships with father-figures; because of their mistrust of, and hostility toward, older males, they are also able to terminate such relationships, as they must in their business careers to obtain the maximum advantage from them.

Later in life they are able to continue relating themselves easily to figures of authority, never too close for disattachment when necessary—never too far away when continuity and closeness are necessary for advancement. How this ability functions in the career of a highly successful leader is illustrated by one of them:

"Right after I arrived on the job I met the boss. That made all the difference! From then on I was on the way up.

"He took an interest in me. The boss and I admired each other; it was a case of mutual respect. You can't look down on a person and create that atmosphere. But the most wonderful thing is to have started with nothing and to have made it together, with my wife.

"I moved up with the boss. He was vice president of North American when I became superintendent. I learned much of what I know about business from him when I became his assistant. I'd have always been with North American but the president and the boss didn't get along. I decided to get out on my own and with two other fellows organized my own company. We almost went broke, but we worked like hell and after a while we caught on and in time expanded and took on new activities. We made money and began to develop a wonderful team of young men. Then my partners retired and I bought them out. All through the years I saw the boss. In fact, before I left we had a talk. He and I discussed our philosophy of the lumber business and business and industry in general. This is the philosophy that finally made North American successful.

"I promised the boss then that if ever there was a right time and a good opportunity I'd still be interested in North American. Well, my business went along and developed, but it was never big enough to carry out the dream the boss and I had. Finally, he got to be president and had complete charge of everything that went on at North American. He called me when he knew he was set for action. All he said was, 'Jim, I think it's time for you and me to get together.' I said okay.

"We were able to work out a deal. North American would take over my outfit on a stock deal and I and my men would come in with him. That was in the early thirties. I came in as a vice president and special assistant to the boss.

"We started immediately putting the principles of our philosophy into action, and I had the opportunity to carry them out directly because the boss trusted me and had to give his attention to other matters. North American grew by leaps and bounds. We spread everywhere and into everything. We gave our customers the best in every way. We soon moved past all of our competitors.

"The boss was the greatest thing that ever happened in my career. When the boss retired the board made me president."

When the interviewer commented on his successful career, this man replied: "I don't think it has been a phenomenal career. I don't put it in those terms. I don't think about it—I just go about my affairs. I don't speculate on it. . . . No, I was never anxious about a promotion; I can truthfully say that. Maybe my association with the boss has something to do with that: as long as he was secure, I felt I was."

Some of the elements of the process of mobility have come into focus. The mobile man must be able to depart: that is, he must maintain a substantial emotional distance from people, and not become deeply involved with them or committed to them; and he must be an energetic person and one who can focus his energy on a single goal. There has probably been in his life a basic and deep experience of separation and loss, that sets this system in motion in terms of his family of birth and his feelings toward his primary love objects, his parents. He must be ready to detach himself, and in moving have no continuing concern for the past.

And what of the arrival? The mobile man in each of these continuing moves must, it seems, be accurate and realistic as he looks at the world around him. He must be able to select his central goals, and drive to them with a total concentration of energy. He must be an attractive person, one who appeals to other people, and one who wants, and is able, to relate to them readily (but always with the underlying reservations that permit perpetuation of his movement). He must be a man who has early been convinced of the fact that through his own efforts, and despite disadvantages, he can achieve some of the goals he sets himself.

All of these characteristics clearly can be present only at an optimal rather than maximal level. Many of the commonly held beliefs about mobile men are in fact caricatures of their real attitudes and behaviors. For example, the mobile man is commonly portrayed as a fiercely competitive man, ever alert for opportunities not only to achieve his goal but more especially to hurt someone else in the process. While it is quite true that the careers of each of the men interviewed must have been built on the bodies of other men who did not succeed, there is no evidence of deep-seated need to hurt their fellows. Rather, they appear to be oblivious of this kind of problem, which illustrates again their single-mindedness. These are not men who are distracted into personal duels, for they do not allow themselves to become so involved with others. At the same time, they are not men who know guilt. The distractions of consideration for others, of weighing the potential damage to others of a contemplated move, do not enter into their calculations.

The mobile man is sometimes carelessly portrayed as a gambler, as a person always willing to take a chance. In this view the successfully mobile man is the occasional winner in the great game of careers. Nothing could be further from the facts. Hayes remarks at one point, for example, "I don't worry. Things always work out all right. As for worrying before decisions, we're pretty sure of ourselves before we go into anything. It's important to know for sure you can do anything you start out to do." This is not the remark of a gambler, but of a determined and realistic man who sets goals consistent with his abilities at a given point in time and then drives hard to reach them.

It is with this order of psychological equipment that these men make their moves. The system seems to work rather smoothly. But there is a great and expensive flaw, for the cycle of departing and arriving and departing has no end. It might be described by a hostile viewer as a nightmare with the script written by Gertrude Stein. What is the point at which these men can stop, look back, and announce to themselves and their world that they have completed this long journey, that they will rest now? There does not seem to be such a point, for an essential part of the system is the need for constant demonstration of one's adequacy, for reiterated proof of one's independence.

5

Success, Failure, and Personality

The man we called Donald Hayes is one of the mobile leaders of American business. Although an individual with his own distinguishing characteristics, he can be taken as typical of men of the mobile elite. His business position is substantial and solid. He looks forward to further business success, and there is every indication he will achieve even higher business status. If he is not quite the leader in his community and social affairs that his business career would seem to warrant, Donald Hayes does not appear troubled by the fact. And if the pursuit of his career has exacted a price in other values, Hayes either is not aware of the price or does not consider it too high.

There is another type among this mobile elite, men who cannot feel the assurance of Hayes in his business and social position, men who face the pressure of failure despite their long and hard-won progress, and who appear tired, isolated, and finished. To understand what men must be like to be mobile, we must understand that group of mobile men who on the brink of final arrival falter and fall back.

One Step ahead of Failure

The history and career of Jeffrey Collins is on the whole similar to that of most mobile men. His father was not a successful man. The elder Mr. Collins owned a farm in Ohio but lost it and moved to a small town where the grandfather owned a second-hand store. After some years of working as a clerk in the store, Mr. Collins tried farming again, but again failed after two years, and once more went back to the job in the store. During this period, when Jeffrey Collins was eleven, he began to work at odd jobs and delivered papers to help support the family. There followed a succession of after-school and summertime jobs until high school graduation when he went to work in a factory on the assembly line.

A period in the army during the First World War seemed to provide the critical break in Collins' career, for he left home to enlist and during his period of service managed to obtain a commission by studying intensively for the examinations for officer training and successfully passing them. "After my experience in the army, I realized the opportunities were not in my home town, and I sort of swore an oath to myself never to go back." He took a job as office boy in a manufacturing plant elsewhere, and worked in a variety of jobs in this and another firm for the next thirteen years.

A chance meeting, through an introduction by older friends, brought Mr. Collins to the attention of an older man who was in the process of setting up an insurance company. Offered a job, Collins accepted, and moved to Cincinnati to work for this new firm. He traveled for a time, worked in the office for a time, and within six years was promoted to vice president of what had become a leading firm in its field.

Many other moves and changes went with this rapid career advancement of Jeffrey Collins, of course. From the small Ohio town he had moved through a number of residences to an expensive suburb of Cincinnati. He owned a twelve-room home there, and became active in community affairs. He worked as a fund-raiser, and then on the board of the local Red Cross, and he and his wife joined the Plank and Tap, a high-status club with limited membership. Mrs. Collins busied herself in community affairs as well, becoming president for a time of the suburban Women's Club.

This is in brief outline a history of movement, change, and

achievement similar to most of the mobile elite. At the same time, this career must have contained the elements that set it off from the majority of the mobile elite, for at the present time Jeffrey Collins may serve as an example of the mobile man who is finally defeated.

About two years ago Collins' business position was taken away from him. He kept the title, and presumably the salary, but found a major part of his responsibility and authority removed. At the time of the interview, the Collinses no longer had the house in the suburb, but were living in a five-room apartment in the city, in an old but respectable apartment neighborhood. The Collinses have dropped their club membership because the group was "too crowded," and Mr. Collins indicated that his community activities had terminated during the past several years. In addition, Mrs. Collins has dropped her club activities because "I don't like women's clubs."

No doubt as a result of some or all of these changes, Mr. Collins greeted the interviewer by saying, "Do you feel you have such a man as you are looking for in me?" That is, he had come to doubt his own success, although the measure of it was in both his position and his prestige as compared with his past. Immediately, he indicated his present uncertainty. "In two or three years I expect to make a change. I'm going to do some of the things I've wanted to do all these years and not had time for." He has already informed the president of the firm of his desire to leave the company as soon as it can be arranged, he told the interviewer. A further measure of Mr. Collins' present lack of self-confidence was provided by the fact that he felt it necessary to clear with the president of the firm before agreeing to an interview, a step most of the other men studied did not feel necessary.

Altogether the success and prestige Jeffrey Collins acquired at such cost to himself and with enormous labor and tenacity appear to be melting away. His social memberships, as well as those of his wife, the home he acquired, and even the job position he attained, all are dwindling. This is not the case of a worn-out old man, at least in years, for Collins is only fifty-four years old. But the steady upward curve of his career, maintained over a period of more than thirty years, suddenly dipped and seems to be directed steadily downward.

Collins is a rather sad figure now. He is somewhat bitter over his present status—"I think there should have been more recognition of those who helped get the company on its feet." Something of the inevitable loneliness of such a man who has been mobile and left people behind, and now is himself left, comes through. "We don't know people much around here yet." And, "We don't have *close* friends, but it's awfully good to run into old friends when you're out of town and take up where you left off! You could almost say my friends are in steps." Fatigue finds expression as Collins describes an ideal vacation—"one where I can get far away from competition."

To search out the total answer to this man's career would no doubt require detailed knowledge of the business he worked in, his competitors, his approach to his work and his life, and much information beyond that available through this study. He provides an important type of contrast to that mobile man whose career curve continues upward. In light of what has already been seen of the mobile man, what is there in what we know of Collins' career and personality that makes him at once similar to, yet different from, the others?

Collins provides an important clue to one point of difference when he says to the interviewer, "A fast-growing company can bring problems, and sometimes I think I should have left after getting the experience. But I didn't have the formal education to help me in much except selling, and I didn't want to have to travel."

Two elements in this remark are important: first, the reference to an inability or failure to move from the company or to travel; and, second, the uncertainty about his abilities and goals implied in the reference to lack of education. The central fact in the lives of these men is movement, and, as we saw in the case of

Donald Hayes, this means detaching oneself from people and places in a continual sequence and driving on for ever new or renewed goals. The whole process of mobility requires a subtle balance between this drive for independence, withdrawal, and departure, and the opposing and necessary need to attach to others, and be respected and honored by them. A successfully mobile man like Donald Hayes is able to maintain this balance—to work with people and be attractive to them, yet leave them behind without guilt or regret.

The difference between Jeffrey Collins and those mobile men whose mobility drive continues is illustrated by his relations with other men. We have noticed that most of the men established themselves in a protégé relationship with an older man who provided a model for them and also rewarded them during their training period. It is a requisite of this protégé system that the model be left behind, without a continuing attachment. The man who served as a model for Collins, the president of his firm, was a person he could not leave. When he remarks that "I think I should have left after getting the experience . . ." he is doubtless correct. For to adopt a new role as a senior man, and to realize the training fully, it would be necessary for him to leave this relationship behind and use the experience, with all its ramifications, in a new situation.

Collins required a subordinate and protected relationship. Moreover, he was not able to sustain the constant departures that continued mobility required. As a result, he remained in a situation that finally defeated him.

Closely related to this factor in Collins' career is the other element of his remark, his regret over his lack of formal training. Repeatedly in the interview he points up the difference between himself and others in the firm in education, and his wife remarked, "The Phi Beta Kappa keys and fraternity pins gave him a large-sized inferiority complex." Underlying this expression of lack of self-confidence for Jeffrey Collins is the fact that, while he rejected the life and status and behavior of his parents, he was not able to set clearly for himself, as an independent person, the goals of his life.

The dual elements of dependence on others and reluctance to set personal goals are both commented on in the TAT analysis. Of course, the strength of these tendencies in Jeffrey Collins should not be overestimated. Like all of the mobile men studied he is intelligent, decisive, and direct. Far more than most persons he is independent and self-directing. He was able to leave the home and for a long time sustain the drive that originally caused him to be a hard-working, self-directing business man. However, two essential elements in occupational mobility—the energy and will to sustain the continual departures mobility prescribes, and the self-direction and independence—must be present in large degree and vitally maintained throughout the career. When the opposite trends to affiliate with other people and become close and dependent on them find too great expression, the chances for failure in the mobility process are greatly increased and result in men like Jeffrey Collins.

The history of this man illustrates that the process of social mobility is enormously demanding of the energies of able men. When the personality dynamics of the individual are not adjusted to these demands, he becomes enervated and, in middle years, becomes fatigued and dull. The whole process of his career turns back on itself to leave an empty and regretful individual, lonely and withdrawn.

Walter Evans: Free, Autonomous, but Isolated

The study of the mobile leader has so far emphasized two groups of men—the central and most numerous group, in whom the qualities necessary for mobility are present, with an optimal balance of the personality characteristics that make for successful mobility; and the group illustrated by Jeffrey Collins where the necessary qualities are not sustained and kept in balance, and ultimate defeat results.

A third group in the mobile elite is perhaps the most dramatic and striking in history and personality, for the need to be mobile and to be detached from people and places occurs here in an extreme form. This group too is self-defeating, but in a different way from Jeffrey Collins. All of these men have been occupationally mobile, to an extreme degree. All have come a long way to their present business and economic positions. But as the case of Donald Hayes suggested, and Jeffrey Collins further indicated, this process of mobility has many of the components of self-destruction in it.

In order to achieve solid position at high levels of our society it is necessary not only to be mobile in job and income, but to re-express this new status in terms of manner of living and social relationships acceptable to ever higher social strata. To arrive at the final and stable high status these men aspire to, they and their families must be accepted into, and become part of, the community of highly placed, prestigeful, and powerful members of their society. As we have seen, all of these mobile men, as a necessary part of the equipment that makes it possible for them to be mobile and leave people behind without fear or regret, have difficulty in easily relating themselves to others over a period of time. They have difficulty in accepting and imposing the kinds of reciprocal obligations that close friendship and intimate social contacts imply. They typically are isolated men; in only the exceptional case, not so far considered, do they achieve in all respects the kind of status and prestige they aspire to.

This characteristic, the need to remain uninvolved with and detached from others, finds its extreme expression in men like Walter Evans. The history and personality of this man provide a picture of the genesis and outcomes of the mobility sequence when carried very nearly to its limits, within the overall compass of successful movement.

All of the dissociation from the past, both social and spatial, characteristic of the mobile man, is markedly present in Evans' history. "Mother was left an orphan when she was small and was raised by some neighbors. My father was left an orphan too, and was raised by a brother and his wife." As to spatial movement, frequent changes in location are among his earliest memories. "We moved thirteen times in fifteen years always to a new home Dad had just built. He would sell it at a profit and move on. But it was hard on the furniture, and it was hard on Mother. The only reason Dad quit was that she just couldn't take it any more."

Evans' father was a pipe-fitter by trade and the family was brought up in South Bend, Indiana. As with the other mobile men, the mother is the primary source of the training necessary for later mobility aspirations. "Dad's always been a hard worker. He likes to work, and has a lot of ability, but he just lost his confidence due to an accident. Besides, it was awfully hard for Dad to change. Maybe he was more stubborn than I am. I have changed and have been able to adjust myself to the trend of the times and Dad wasn't able to do that. Perhaps the main reason Dad quit work in the tire company we had was because Mother made him clean up before he came home. She always had great ideas. The grocery and food business she considered degrading. I can't figure out where she got those notions. I had to take piano lessons from the best teacher around." Again, like most of these men he says, "I'm more like my mother."

Walter Evans doesn't express his feelings about his father quite so openly as some of these men, but they can be read between the lines of his remarks. "After Dad had his accident, he slipped fast. The last thirty years he's just made a living. Yes, actually I've done very much better than Dad did. There were years during the twenties when he applied for job after job, and he'd be passed along, but before he was they'd always find out where I was and what I was doing. Naturally they were more interested in a younger man, and I had a reputation by then. It got so I hated to see him go see anybody who knew both of us."

Evans is now executive vice president of a nation-wide chain of restaurants. He hasn't stopped moving. "I won't stay here long at the present level. I should be president of the company in about two years. I'll test them out on it and if I don't think I'll get it

I'll start to look around. I feel I could run any business better than it's being run now. I wouldn't hesitate to take over the presidency of General Motors tomorrow." He has no qualms about moving. "If I felt a move was the best thing, we moved. Sometimes Mrs. Evans didn't know about it until the day before the move but she never objected."

Evans is another of these mobile men, self-confident, hard-driving, from a background typical of his kind. He's come a long way and, like Donald Hayes but unlike Jeffrey Collins, he's still moving. But in one respect he is different, for in all his relations with others he is quite evidently unpleasant, overbearing, and aggressive. Evans talked about his fellow executives—"I lie awake nights thinking of ways in which the firm can get ahead over night. It's easy as falling off a log—they're stupid guys, the ones I work with and the leaders of competitive companies." Asked if any of the men he works with are close friends, he said, "Who has any good friends? Maybe one or two but if I left the present company I'd find new ones and the old ones would be forgotten. So would I. Oh, sure, I have plenty of friends. I could call any bank president in St. Louis and you'd have dinner with him because of my friendship with him. But it doesn't mean anything. I learned a long time ago not to form close attachments. It's easier to fire the guy when you are moved ahead of him. I think that's very important. Yet I'm friendly. I make a point of never hurting anyone unnecessarily but rather try to make any place better for my having been there." Evans later gave an interesting example of his kind of friendship: "This guy got me a job with this company. He knew me and knew what I can do." Asked if he sees this man now, Evans replied, "Yes, maybe once a year. When he's in trouble he calls. But he's not with the company any more; he didn't seem to fit into the business. He's a promoter actually. He does a terrific job as long as he can get somebody else to do the work. That's why I didn't follow him except when he fit into *my* picture."

The approach of this man to his home life and his wife's role in his career is summed up by him—"I've read the magazine articles that say a man should marry the girl with more of everything than he has, that through her contacts with other wives he can get ahead. I've proved that this is not necessarily true and should write an article of my own to show how. Instead of marrying up, I married down. My wife had less of everything, money and contacts even, than I had. I've kept my home life completely separated from business always. My wife has never met the business associates' wives and never will if I can help it."

Even his brother fails to escape the general contempt and superiority Evans expresses toward those around him. "My brother has an awfully good time staying out of jail. He went one year to the university before he was kicked out. He's smart as a whip and has a very good mind but we never know whether his job or his wife is permanent or not. Sometimes he's fired and sometimes he quits. Sometimes he does things just a little bit shady. He should have been encouraged to work instead of being pampered the way he was."

These strong feelings of aggressiveness and superiority hardly need to be analyzed. In all his relations with other people, whoever they may be, Evans portrays himself as a tough, able, self-sufficient person. He doubtless is to a considerable degree. The braggadocio in his remarks and the fact that he felt compelled to portray himself in this way to a stranger, the vehemence, and reiteration cause wonder. A partial answer can be gathered from the report of the TAT analyst:

The underlying characteristic of Evans' approach to the world is his drive to be free of all kinds of restrictions, personal or moral. For example, in his dealings with other people, particularly with women, his first impulse is to lash out, to find their weak spots and use this knowledge to assert his own dominance. At the same time he is very aware of appearances and sensitive to the way in which his behavior is seen and judged by others. As a result, in order to keep up appearances and avoid the punishment that might result from this behavior, he tries to hold himself in and keep from exceeding the bounds of propriety in his behavior toward others.

Evans is not simply an amoral man. [Although he so describes himself, for in the interview he says, "I'd rather read a biography of Dillinger than a light novel. Maybe you don't think much of Dillinger but he was successful in what he attempted."] However, he is made uncomfortable by moral restrictions and feels deeply that morality serves to defeat its possessor. For example, he says of one character, "She's too steeped in her ideals of what's right and wrong. They are too deeply beaten into her. It would keep her from ever being noticed." We may take this to be an expression of his own feelings toward the moral code he has been trained in by his parents, and his conscious reaction from that code.

As with his morality, so with Evans' reaction to other people. He is a man who must, to accomplish his goals, feel that he is free of other persons. He requires a specific goal, and will work most effectively when he feels he can concentrate absolutely all his attention, thought, and efforts on that goal. Rules and people, morals and affections, are constricting and dangerous. They are both tempting and weakening, and serve to prevent the independence and freedom from his situation that Evans requires.

We cannot know what basic experiences of treachery, loss, or betrayal produced this kind of a man. It is clear, though, that while Evans learned the necessity of working hard to gain his ends, he has also been deeply impressed with the fact that a man must trust no one, and be close to no one. Had his experience of loss or betrayal, whatever its nature, been more drastic, or had his parents—his mother, in particular—provided less reassurance and stability to him, Evans' career might have been quite different from that of the successful business man. In fact, however, the kind of psychological equipment that he has is much to his advantage in his career, for it enables him to carry through to a maximal degree the kind of departing and arriving necessary to mobility.

Evans has many examples and proofs to reinforce his basic feeling toward other people and other men in particular. He recounted this story. "There was a principal at the high school who taught me not to trust people, and some of the things in handling people I don't trust. I disliked him very much. He was very partial. He had the feeling that certain people in certain walks of life could help him. I said to myself, 'You've got a fight on your hands that you don't fight with your fists.' And I did it. That's what I mean by learning to be a man. If somebody does something to me I'll take care of it if it takes fifty years." At another point, Evans described a time in his career when "I first went into business with a friend, but we agreed to disagree. I ducked and went into the grocery business—my father and me. It was all right except that Dad didn't particularly like it, and left me holding the bag." Repeatedly in his career, Evans finds occasion to describe himself as betrayed or abandoned or attacked by older men, and draws the moral of absolute self-sufficiency.

In the TAT analysis the following attitudes are revealed:

Evans has no difficulty in maintaining his feelings of superiority and distance from women, including the mother. Sexuality is intriguing, amusing, and necessary, but he does not get so involved as to develop a close attachment to any woman as a result of sexual needs. Rather he will treat women either as sexual objects—and therefore easily dealt with and disposed of—or as social objects, to be used in establishing the kind of social milieu he feels necessary to his career.

In his relations with men, however, Evans has a good deal more difficulty in maintaining the high degree of freedom and independence and dominance he needs to be comfortable. His approach to other men is hesitant, and he feels uncertain of himself in relation to them. He mistrusts other men, feels they are thinking ahead of him, and using him rather than his being in a dominant position. This causes him considerable dis-ease and in defense he seeks to establish his own individuality distinct from them. Specifically in terms of his father, Evans does not see his father as really part of the family and avoids contact with him in a family situation. In a man-to-man relationship he seems to feel that his father is potentially stronger than he, definitely not a helpful person, but rather a person who is amused and gratified by the difficulties his son gets into. This mistrust of the father is reflected in his attitude toward other males, and gives rise in behavior to the cold and calculating interaction with other men that Evans displays.

Evans is not the tough, independent, and ruthless person he appears to be. He is a man who is afraid of being placed in a position of dependence or weakness toward others; to avoid this, he tries to deny his basically strong morality and becomes immoral. In his relations with other people he becomes hostile and distant, in fear of the weakness that he feels close relations with people will bring.

This type of man is not common in the mobile group. His aggression and distance from others frequently antagonize associates and make him a vulnerable target for competitors and disturbing in organizations. No doubt success on the part of these men calls for exceptional control of feelings and a high level of abilities to compensate for the possible damage they do to their associates.

In terms of social mobility, however, the important fact to keep in mind is that this type of man is placed in a dilemma by his mobility. The set of feelings and attitudes toward others that Walter Evans displays represents in somewhat extreme form the "departure" aspect of the typically mobile man. These attitudes facilitate his personal adjustment to this difficult mobility process; but, at the same time, they make it impossible for him to achieve a high level of social status in both the occupational and social hierarchies. The very qualities that make for rapid movement, ready departure, and easy accommodation to ceaseless and drastic change make it impossible for these men, when higher occupational positions are attained, to build for themselves and their families the social relations that solid status in their communities requires. Even to move to the highest occupational levels they find themselves caught in the system of their own making. Evans realizes this dimly. His wife is isolated from him, his position, and its social correlates. She remains the naïve, poorly educated, socially withdrawn person he married down to, as he puts it. Her present role is of his making, for it is the way he must have his wife. Yet—"My wife just plain don't know what I've done. She'd be more interested in me being a $60-a-week grocery store clerk and be home. It would be a wonderful deal if she could work well with the other wives. My getting the presidency would be easy then."

The attitude of Walter Evans toward his wife and family illustrates an important aspect in the lives of these mobile men. They do not travel alone. Accompanying them, and coming to terms with the mobility process somehow, are their wives and children. The attitudes they reveal toward their families give insight into the kinds of men they are and the way in which they see their world.

One central characteristic is their enormous concentration on their careers. All of these mobile men show up in the interviews to be devoting almost all of their energies to the forwarding of their business careers, the company they are with, and their position in the company. This fact becomes apparent in men like Jeffrey Collins who, when put in a limited business position, have little or nothing else to do, no non-business interests or activities to turn to, and who do not seem to be able to refocus their energies. This group of men seem to be listless and apathetic, defeated men.

The concentration on business activities is more apparent in Collins because his business position has lessened. With the other men, however, the fact of this concentration is no less clear. For example, when these mobile men describe their community activities it is in terms of the Chamber of Commerce, associations of manufacturers, bankers, or retailers, organizations of specialists such as financial men or production men—in general, groups and organizations that are an immediate extension of the business activities engaged in.

This focusing on the business career extends to those activities that ostensibly lie somewhat outside the immediate business realm, as, for example, running the finance drive for the Red Cross, YMCA, or Community Chest; for such activities are a definite part of a man's job as an executive and are frequently undertaken on explicit or implicit instructions from his company. They do not necessarily represent for these men a felt obligation to the community or an opportunity to participate with a broader social group. Hobbies, sports, and other interests are slighted or ignored. As one said, "Hobbies? I guess my business is my hobby." Even in the choice of vacations business concerns predominate. A dramatic expression of this came in the remark of one mobile man. "Anywhere I go I'm pretty close to my business. There's always a tendency to connect the locality with your business. You can't drive through California without thinking this or that spot would be good for a branch. A long ocean voyage would be ideal because you couldn't establish a branch there." But he doesn't take the ocean voyage.

This driving concentration on the career is necessary to mobility. The task of moving through the business hierarchy is a hard, demanding one, and requires the intense focusing of great interests and energies and skills. We have seen that this is a characteristic of these men, the ability to focus their energies in this fashion on the tasks they set themselves. Without this capacity they would not have moved as they have.

At the same time, this is the narrowest definition of their task, for they are moving through the total social system—whether or not they realize it. They cannot and do not move alone. In order to reach the goals they set themselves, they must be able to define what they are doing and want to do in broader terms than the immediate job. Again, a basic dilemma and contradiction appear, for this necessary entire concentration on business makes it impossible for them to develop the broader interests and activities necessary to participate with the kinds of people they encounter as they move up in the business hierarchy. (No doubt the many accusations of provincialism and boorishness directed toward the "self-made man" are a direct result of just this problem. To be self-made in the derogatory sense in which it is usually used means that energy and attention have not been given to becoming the more sophisticated and literate person his critics would have him be.)

On the subject of the feelings of these men toward their families, some of their comments reveal how their attitudes toward themselves and their world affect their wives. "My wife is very adaptable. She works out things the way I want them to be. As long as we're together and working together." Another typical remark was, "She doesn't interfere with my business life at all. She's very tolerant of my comings and goings. She had to adapt herself to my necessities."

Even though most of these men are not as vehement in isolating their wives as Walter Evans, they share many basic attitudes. First, the wife must accept and work toward the goals set by the mobile man. She above all must learn to tolerate and even encourage the long hours, many business trips, and frequent moves dictated by the nature of her husband's career needs. She must provide him a base of operations, but a base that is not demanding and that will provide continual support, or, failing that, at least in no way interfere with the problems that he is concerned with.

The wife must not be demanding of her husband, either of his time or of his interest. Manifest by the kind of job concentration these men reveal, even their sexual activity is limited. This tremendous concentration of energy no doubt has its source, to a great extent, in sexual energy. No deflection is tolerated. Repeatedly in the psychological analyses they see sexual relations as limiting, frivolous, and unreal.

Just as they define their own lives within the narrow confines of business activity, so they tend to define their wives' activities narrowly in terms of home and children. However, while they are engaged in continual social learning in the course of their business success, learning different behaviors, tastes, and manners, their wives by the men's very demands are limited to the narrow definition of activity they set for them in the majority of cases. The present activities of the wife of Walter Evans serve as an illustration. This is a woman who is now totally unequipped for the role of wife of the company president. She is unable to function in her role of wife of a substantial and important member of the community.

Few of these men marry women from backgrounds markedly

different from their own. For the most part their wives are from similar, or only slightly better, social and economic backgrounds. They have not had earlier training to equip them to function in a social position corresponding to the present position of their husbands; and they have been prevented by the attitudes of their husbands from learning new social behavior.

In most cases when the husband completes his occupational movement and turns to his wife for the assistance he must have from her to advance socially and consolidate his position, she is unable to help. In the cases of the most successful men, the wives play important roles in facilitating the more substantial social adjustment as they move through the business ranks.

Arrival and Departure

The sons of mobile men are of sufficient interest to be the subject of folklore: "From shirtsleeves to shirtsleeves in three generations." The difficulties encountered by the sons are in no small part created by the attitudes of the mobile fathers. It would hardly seem possible that these men would find time to be interested in their children's activities; this seems well supported in all of the cases. Particularly in the early years of the children's lives, the fathers are almost totally preoccupied with their careers and expect their wives to shield them from the distractions of family problems and activities. Also, because of the way in which they relate themselves to other people, they do not develop close relations with their children. Just as in their attitudes to all persons, they tend to strive to remain free of really close involvement with their offspring.

When interviewed, many of these men, now in maturity, had turned, or been forced to turn, more attention to their children, especially their sons. In many cases they express bewilderment, or lack of understanding, or real concern. One father seems puzzled. "Jack went out to California to visit his sister and stayed down there. He opened up a small store where he sells books and pictures. He's doing very well; he's more like his mother—likes nice things and art and so forth. I never had much of a flair for that. When he was thinking of starting a book store I didn't think it was too good an idea. I thought he ought to get something more solid. But that's what he wanted, so I didn't interfere. I never did have too much time to devote to my son and daughter."

The disquiet and regret of this father, when speaking of his son, are echoed by others: "He's had a lot more advantages than I had. He's had a good education and a good home life with few worries. He is like me in that he likes people and can get along with them. But I don't think he has the ambition I had when I was his age. . . ." "My son is a very good student but he doesn't have any desire or urge toward athletics or group activities. He always preferred to sit and read. He doesn't seem to have any get-up and go to him. . . . If we could only implant that urge or drive."

Some of the sons seem to have little desire to follow the father in his business, although others do so successfully. Others are successfully engaged in the professions or in such special fields as personnel work and industrial engineering.

In most instances the age of the son precludes testing out the "shirtsleeves to shirtsleeves" argument. There does seem to be a substantial basis, judging from the comments of the parents about their sons, for the belief in the justness of the saying. There can be no doubt that the attitude of these men toward their sons is a major factor in the difficulties their sons experience in adjusting to adult life. The mobile man is indifferent to his son, hardly aware of his presence, for a greater part of the time. But he is also demanding of his son, expects him to be able and ambitious. He expects his son, who has been brought up in comfortable circumstances, to feel the same urgency about his future and his career as the father did. Like any father, he looks to his son to share his view of the world. The mobile father seldom remembers that the world in which his son is living, both socially and economically, is removed from the world the father was born into.

The men speak for themselves. Here are two mobile men,

fathers describing their sons, and revealing as they do their own inappropriate expectations and demands, and the results in their sons' behavior of the pressure they have exerted on them.

"My son has shown signs of not being too hard a worker. He wants the best things in life, but he's not willing to work for them. He has proven that he has definite characteristics that are good. When he sets his mind to it he does it. He's similar to my wife to some extent. I mean, in appearance he is like her, but that's as far as it goes. . . ." Later: "My son took advantage of my being away a lot and when I'd return after being away I was bound to be more lenient. You're bound to lose a certain control, influence. That's one of the penalties you have to pay for moving and being in sales work."

"We don't understand our boy; I guess no parent understands his child. He's not a student, but he's a good kid. Never was in any trouble." What plans do you have for him? "To grow up and be a useful citizen. We want him to do what he wants to do. I've tried to interest him in various things. He wants to stay out of the army, so he's in school now. He doesn't know what he wants to do. That's the problem with him. I can't understand it."

Like all men, the men of the mobile business elite are unique individuals, with characteristics that set them apart from each other. One man uses golf as a business method and technique; another has no use for hobbies or sports of any sort. One treats women as useful but unimportant objects; another avoids women; yet another is courtly and mannered toward women. Some of these men believe children are spoiled by being supported through college; others are rather lavish in bestowing gifts on their children.

For all these considerable variations, no less than would be found among most groups of men of similar background, histories, and careers, there are similarities that set this group apart in many ways. When these similarities are seen against the background of their lives, it is clear that the personality factors held in common have played an important role in their mobility. Having looked more closely at a few of the mobile men, we will sum up certain of the qualities they have in common.

Their lives have a repeated theme which provides a basic rhythm to their histories. This theme is the recurrent departing and arriving and departing in every aspect of their lives. This is the common element, and the necessary element, to this kind of career and history. To achieve mobility each of these men has, as an underlying component of his personality, attitudes toward his world and the people in it that make these departures and arrivals possible.

The system of movement is frequently set in motion, it seems, by a loss—the death of a parent, severe illness of a parent, repeated changes in the home, sudden changes in ways of living. This experience no doubt provides the basis for the first, most difficult, and most important departure, the break of the close and intimate ties with the parents. Unless this is achieved, no mobility is possible. It is also clear that this break is primarily with the father, who is the person whom they lose, or who abandons them.

At the same time, the shock of this initial experience, whatever it might be, must be alleviated by positive feelings and experiences in order for these men to be productive and useful persons in our society. Here the figure of the mother is important, for without exception the mother is singled out as the person who has trained them, who provides them with a sense of a larger and different world from that in which they live, and who is the close and stable figure in the family. She is at the same time a controlling figure. While they feel some guilt over leaving the mother, they are not able to accept or tolerate the control she might exert over them. They are men who must feel that they can withdraw from other people at their own convenience.

This set of attitudes toward other people, particularly males, makes it possible for the mobile men to adopt and use to their advantage the important protégé relationship that plays such a large role in their later training. It is the mothers of these men who initially provide them with the notion that by dint of hard work and personal effort they can achieve goals they set themselves. Yet it seems likely that this training must be reinforced by later experiences to provide the kind of assurance and faith that makes the mobile man go through the long and often painful training years, the lean years, before he can realize tangible rewards for his efforts and training.

With the need and ability to leave persons and relate again to new friends and co-workers who are in turn left for yet another group, the mobile men must have a strong sense that the world they live in can be shaped to some extent by their individual efforts. No doubt this is a part of the total culture which has as a basic tenet the belief that events and circumstances are malleable and that destinies may be shaped. Remembering that these are men from lower backgrounds socially and economically, we find it remarkable that they have acquired and retained this belief in the efficacy of skill, training, and hard work. Without this belief they would give way to indifference and apathy, and the energy would be dissipated. It would seem that, in addition to reinforcements of the culture in which they live, the basis for this belief in their capacities must come from the mother, and be reconfirmed definitely by later experiences in school, play, and early in their job careers.

No doubt these two elements, the capacity to leave, arrive, and leave again, and the unconscious faith in the malleability of their world, are a substratum of attitudes. Along with these common characteristics the mobile men are alike in other important respects. They share a high level of energy, an ability to expend enormous effort on achieving a desired end. This factor is closely related to the capacity for complete concentration. To them the career and its immediate environs are all that matter. They can focus their entire selves on their job, to the exclusion of all other matters, daydreams, family, social life, or any extra interests that might intrude. Coupled with, and partly a result of, their belief in the efficacy of hard work to gain reward, this provides them a powerful advantage over less energetic competitors.

Many other psychological factors are shared by the men of the mobile elite. They are not brilliant men, usually, but they do have an intelligence level substantially above average. More interesting is their utter realism. Their judgments are quick, tough, and accurate. They do not become distracted. They do not mistake some minor issue for the main problem as it concerns them, nor do they wander from this main problem. They see people accurately with no sentimentality. This is not a meanness but a kind of cold hard vision, always directed by the overriding need to work problems through to solutions, to work situations through to a rewarding conclusion.

All of these characteristics are important to the mobility process they are engaged in. These men are quick to pick up cues. They can move into new situations successfully without letting themselves get involved prematurely. They can approach people easily, but always with an inner reservation that leaves them free to move out and on when they need to.

All of these psychological characteristics, however, are effective only if set in the context of the basic ability to depart and arrive and depart that mobility demands. The emotional approach of these men to other people is essential to their successful exploration of their other capacities to advance their mobility. This emotional approach is also the basic cause of the price they pay for mobility—isolation, fatigue, and the inability to make their final arrival in a high-status community position.

This section of the study of the mobile business elite has emphasized the part that personality plays in their careers. This should not indicate that personality factors are in any sense the cause of social mobility in American business or that personality factors in some sense control business mobility. The process of mobility is complex; it could not be expected that any one set of factors could cause or maintain it.

All of the cases just presented and this summary comprise an analysis of the mobility process in terms of the individual. The role of individual personality and individual differences has been emphasized. Yet the business system and its operations play a crucial role in the process. Our expanding economy and continuing growth of business and industry certainly play a major part in making men mobile. The elaborate selection and training programs, developed by business and industry, facilitate mobility.

The American educational system also plays its part. Much attention is paid, justifiably and correctly, to the fact that movement through the business hierarchy is not equitable, and studies have demonstrated the inequities of our school systems in their treatment of persons from lower socio-economic backgrounds. Yet the school system contains important components that make it possible for potentially mobile youths to acquire the training, both technical and social, they must have to realize their potential. Free public education, scholarships of all descriptions offered by various groups, the tax-supported state universities, and more recently the GI Bill have all helped the educational system to play some part in the mobility process.

Another major factor in mobility apart from personality factors is the American Dream itself; belief in it plays an important part in making its realization possible. A person in any society who is convinced that the social system he lives in is fixed and immutable, and that his place in that system is inevitable, proper, and right, is unable, whatever his personality may be, to be mobile. The belief in the malleability of the social world around one is not universal in our society, but a rich complex of symbols and ritual provides constant restatement of the American Dream in terms that all Americans can understand. Without such a cultural heritage no man would be mobile.

The widest variety of additional factors enters into the mobility these men have experienced. The kinds of women they marry, their health, no doubt their physical appearance, a whole complex of factors must come together to cause this social phenomenon. Surely, too, chance must be assigned some role.

To determine the part that the business system, the educational system, our culturally given beliefs, and all other factors play in social mobility would require a detailed and exhaustive examination. Each factor plays its part and all must come together in combination to make mobility possible. In this interacting system of causes, personality is one factor.

Until now we have dealt with the business leader and the facts of his business career. Although by necessity we have examined the occupation of the father and certain other facts having to do with the personality and origin of the leader, his wife and family have not greatly concerned us. Since the wife plays an important part in the career of most men and since marrying a woman above, below, or at his own level not only has consequences for the career of the leader but for the society as a whole, we shall in the next two chapters examine the facts about, and meanings of, the wives of the business men. We shall examine the wives' social backgrounds first and, in the chapter following the next, find out what roles the wives play and how their private worlds relate to the lives and careers of their husbands.

6

The Wives
of Ambitious Men

The Social Background of the Wives

From the moment of her marriage to John Jacob O'Flaherty, Margaret shared and participated in his "rags to riches" career. She not only loved him, bore his children, and was the good wife who refreshed and strengthened him during periods of crisis and in times of momentary defeat, but advised and counseled him— though never about his business problems. When occasion demanded she scolded him, particularly when Jake became "too lofty and domineering for his own good," telling him he wore ordinary pants like all other men, not the robe of a cardinal. She was an able hostess and was involved in many philanthropies and civic organizations. Jake relied on her shrewd comments about their friends and their personalities, but they never discussed his business and political associates.

Margaret O'Flaherty was the daughter of a wealthy engineer who became an important executive. She, her sister Anne, and their brothers inherited a large fortune from him. The father had risen from nothing to the presidency and control of a building and construction corporation that spread throughout the Eastern states. It was agreed when they were married that Margaret would not receive help from her family. Jake's self-confidence and pride prevented this. Not until he himself had risen to power and wealth and long after the death of her father did the O'Flaherty sons receive their inheritance from the grandfather's estate.

Although Jake is a self-made man, his wife's social background, the role she plays as his able companion, and the friendly, outgoing person she has been throughout the ups and downs of Jake's career have contributed greatly to his advancement. "She's been a wonderful partner on my roller coaster," Jake likes to say; "up or down, tough or easy, she's never been scared."

But just what have Mrs. O'Flaherty and the wives of other business leaders contributed to their husbands' careers? What has been the effect of their economic and social backgrounds? Would Jake's career have been the same if his wife had been the daughter of a laborer, defined her role as a housewife, and confined her activities to the home? Clearly, too, the easy, relaxed Margaret who could face the problems that confront all mobile men must have strengthened and helped her husband. Her sister Anne also married well. Her husband is an important banker in New York. Some people say she and Margaret are very alike; others, that they are quite different. Both judgments are right as we shall see later when we compare the two sisters, primarily for the purpose of understanding Mrs. O'Flaherty and what such a wife means to mobile men like Jake.

The wives of business leaders are as diverse in background, experience, and personality as their husbands. To gain some estimation of their significance for our problem, we studied them with several basic questions in mind.

What are the social and economic *backgrounds* of the wives? What kinds of *roles* do women assume when they play their parts (or fail to) in the success stories of the business leaders? What kinds of *persons* are these wives as human beings? How do they relate themselves to their husbands and to their advancement? What do they do and how do they do it? To answer these and other questions we will use evidence from the personal answers of the men and the results of interviewing them about their wives and families. But, most importantly, we will present the life stories told by the wives themselves, as well as the results of the personality tests of the private worlds of these women. Before examining the kinds of personalities and roles played by the wives to evaluate their success or failure in playing their parts, we first present their social and economic backgrounds.

The way the business leader relates to his wife as well as his children, his satisfactions and frustrations, the ease with which he translates economic and pecuniary success into social achievement, "what he brings to the job" every morning and goes home to at night, may vary greatly with the choice he makes in the social and economic background of the woman he marries. Do these men often marry above or below themselves? Did the highly successful men of ambition usually seek and find women to marry from higher social and economic positions very much in the style they sought and acquired their present high positions in the business elite? Did they marry the daughters of big business men or those of the much esteemed professional groups? Or did they more often marry at the lower levels of their own origin and fashion a lifetime career of continuing to advance from there to higher levels, a career in which their wives shared and fought to maintain for themselves and their children the pace set by their husbands?

If sons of the leaders marry only daughters of the same group, then our social-class lines are rigid. Interclass marriage, one of the principal methods by which women advance their status, contributes strongly to the fluidity of our social-class system. Lacking this route to upward movement, the daughters of men from the lower levels would face impossible barriers. The children would have to go outside the circle of family and friends to experience what people from other social and economic levels are as social beings. They would learn to recognize them as outsiders.

But marriage of these sons outside their class helps to keep the social lines of our society flexible. The children of these marriages are nearer all other children, and the family is a more integrated participant in the life of the whole community because the social distance is reduced.

For the social and economic origins of the wife, occupational background was used, as for the business leader, to indicate the family's status. At the two extremes, about half of the wives were from business and professional backgrounds, compared with a slightly higher proportion for the business leaders, and about one sixth of the wives came from the laboring class compared to slightly less for the business leaders.

We of course wanted to learn how the leaders of each occupational background married. All tend to marry a higher proportion

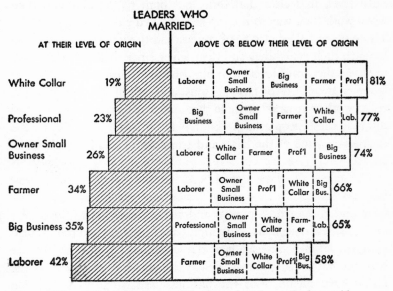

Chart VII.   Who Marries at His Own Level, or Perhaps Above or Below?

NOTE: Only 19 per cent of men born to the white collar class married women of that class and 81 per cent married into the other levels.

of women of their own occupational background than any other (see Chart VII), but they also marry at all other levels, usually in greater proportions at levels nearer to them than at a distance. There was considerable variation among the levels of business leaders for the kinds of marriages they made: the sons of the elite were second only to the sons of laborers in marrying women of the same background as their own; on the other hand, white-collar sons, less than any other, married within their own group—in fact they marry at all other levels in about the same degree as their own. This reinforces the picture we already have of the white-collar group—they seem to be less contained than the others. They are more likely to marry the daughters of laborers than any other class except laborers themselves.

Since most of the business leaders marry at or near their own birth level, it is clear that those not born to the elite and their wives work their way to the top as a married pair (see Chart VII). Those nearest the bottom, of course, had the longest way to travel to reach their goal—they and their wives, since their marriages were made at the lower levels too: almost three fourths of the sons of laborers, two thirds of farmers' sons, and half of the sons of white-collar workers married at these three low occupational levels. Since most of these people have children fairly early, the children too experience some of the trials and triumphs of climbing the social ladder.

The effect of three generations on the marriage of present business leaders shows us how descent and family influence marriage and those who aspire to and achieve such status. Over half of the leaders' sons marry daughters of big business and professional men, the latter being usually at the same social level—the distance is across, rather than down. When the grandfather as well as the father were members of the business leadership the proportion rises from one half to two thirds; only a small fraction marry the daughters of laborers or farmers, and about a fourth marry into the white-collar class. If the grandfather were of the elite but the father had dropped in position to, let us say, the laboring class, only about a fourth of the sons married into the elite; but this is a much higher proportion than the marriages of sons whose grandfathers as well as fathers had been laborers. In general, if the paternal grandfather is of high status, the chances of the son's marrying high status are greater than if the grandfather is of lower status.

Over half of our present business leaders whose grandfathers and fathers were laborers married women whose fathers were laborers,[1] and only one tenth married into the elite. But if the father had risen from his laborer background to become a white-collar worker or small business man, the effect on the present generation is that almost twice as many marry into the elite; and if the father had risen to the elite himself, from his laborer background, the percentage marrying into the elite doubles again. It would seem that a trend to mobility, started in one generation, is sustained and augmented in the next.

"Who" the Women of Different Social Levels Married

We have looked at the kinds of women the business leaders married and found, for example, that they come from all economic levels, in varying proportions. Yet we know that they, like their husbands, are an elite group. Many of them are ambitious women who have used marriage to achieve top status; others, equally ambitious, have taken a slower route and married men "of good prospects" and have risen from economic and social obscurity into the elite. Some have actively helped in this rise to success; others have been passive partners who have, nevertheless, enjoyed the increase in the family's fortunes; and a few have remained behind.

Are the marriages of these women different or the same? Do women of top status tend to marry fewer men from lower levels than from the top levels? Do the daughters of laborers marry up more often than the sons? Do women in the white-collar and small business levels marry men who are above rather than below them?

Most of the women born to the business elite and professional classes married men of this same high-status background: almost two thirds of the women of big business background and about half of those with professional background. They married into the laborer level almost not at all.

At the other extreme, over a third of the daughters of laborers married sons of laborers and made their way with them from the

[1] Warner and Abegglen, *op. cit.*, Ch. VII, "The Marriages of the American Business Elite."

bottom to the top. Next to the group of birth elite, the women of laborer background show the highest proportion of marriages to men of the same origin. Daughters of white-collar and small business men marry less at their own level, and the daughters of farmers more often marry men from the lower levels than the higher.

We wanted to know if the women of this group differed from the men in the way they married so, with a simple statistical device, we compared every type of marriage and found that the women marry up and out of their own levels more than the men, but that the differences are not great. In general, there is a greater tendency for women from the lower levels to marry above themselves and less tendency to marry beneath themselves.

The man who marries the boss's daughter symbolizes some of the conflicting feelings in American life. He is envied by some and scorned by others; he is believed by many to have made an easier road for himself by marrying position, yet he is usually the first to disclaim advantage and, in fact, insist that his way is made harder, that he is constantly under attack to prove his ability.

To test the possible advantage of a man's marrying position, we settled upon one measurement as the best single available indicator: how long did it take him to achieve *entrance* into the business elite from the time he became self-supporting? If his marriage has been of advantage to him in his career, his promotions should be rapid and the time to achieve top position should be shorter; if his marriage has not been of advantage, or of possible disadvantage, the time should be longer.

We found that it took the sons of big business men only 21 years (the mean number of years from the time they became self-supporting) to achieve entrance into the business elite compared with 26 for the sons of laborers. When we introduced the factor of the status of the wife, according to her father's occupational background, we learned that the sons of big business men who married daughters of laborers took 23 years to achieve top position and those who married at their own level took

25 years, that is, about 2 years longer. In fact, marriage outside of their own status worked to the advantage of this top group, for their road to success was a longer one if they married women of their own level.

It took the sons of laborers the same number of years (26) to achieve success if they married at their own level or at the higher level—a little less time if they married the daughters of white-collar workers or farmers or professional men (25). It took sons of farmers 5 years longer if they married at the elite rather than at their own level. It took the sons of the white-collar and professional classes approximately the same length of time whether they married at the top or bottom of the occupational scale.

Clearly if there are advantages to the career in certain types of marriage, they do not lie in marriage into the elite group. This type of marriage undoubtedly brings social advantages that are outside the scope of this study. American business men do not achieve position through marriage; rather, they "get places by doing things."

As far as success is concerned, we have seen that the business man who is foreign-born does well and often excels those whose fathers have been here for many generations. One might argue that these men actually have many obstacles to overcome and the fact of their success is a tribute to their perseverance, ambition, great ability, or many other qualities. A crucial test of how much ethnic status interferes with the career of the foreign-born business man is whom they marry, as compared with marriages of old Americans. Men whose fathers and grandfathers were born in the United States married the daughters of laborers less and the daughters of big business men more than any other group. But here the clear differences stop. For example, first-generation Americans marry into the laboring class more than the foreign-born and into the business elite and professional groups at the same rate. In general, while the old Americans are slightly advantaged, the differences are not great and certainly do not indicate that the foreign-born are deterred by their ethnic status in the types of marriages they make.

Just as ethnic status is believed to interfere with marrying up, so it is often thought that different regions of the country have an advantage or disadvantage. We considered only the amount of in-marriage, or endogamy, of each group by region and found that the average for all occupational backgrounds and all regions of the country is 29 per cent, or 3 in-marriages for every 10. We found that there is more *out*-marriage in the Far West, including the Mountain and Pacific Coast regions, and a greater tendency in the East, including New England and the Middle and South Atlantic states, to in-marriages.

Education, Marriage, and Occupational Mobility

We have been looking at a number of factors in the life careers of our business leaders that should now be brought into focus at the same time to see if they form some kind of meaningful pattern. We know that a high percentage of our business leaders are college graduates—some because they come from the kind of background that assumes college education for its children, others because a college education was part of the plan to reach the career goal. We have looked at marriage first from the point of view of the husband, then of the wife, and learned that many men and women of low or moderate status marry at the same level and advance with their mates to high status, that a large percentage born to the elite marry at this level, that a small but important group marry down. Just as there were no rigid barriers to prevent mobile men from rising in their careers, so there were no barriers in the kinds of marriages they or their wives could make, and no barriers in the kinds of lives they could fashion for themselves as marriage partners.

Let us now consider together these factors of occupational background, education, and marriage. How does education fit into the marriage picture? Do educated men more often marry women of higher occupational background than their less educated competitors? Does college education increase the likelihood of a man's marrying a woman of superior status? Do men of low educational attainment marry women from lower occupational categories? Briefly, how does a man's education affect his choice of a mate— or how he is chosen?

Men who had graduated from college married women of the higher business group in greater proportion than any other (one fourth), with daughters of professional men next (one fifth), and so on down the line in diminishing numbers. Marriages to the elite and professional groups were higher and marriages to daughters of laborers were lower for college graduates than for any other group. Conversely, the men who did not graduate from high school married the daughters of laborers more than those of any other occupation—one third of their marriages were at this level; and they married the daughters of professional men least—7 out of every 100 were at this level and 10 out of 100 were marriages to big business background.

Now we want to add the factor of the occupational background of the business leader to the relationship of marriage and education. Do the sons of laborers, when they are college trained, marry women of higher status in the same way as the sons of small business men who are also college trained?

College education for the sons of laborers lessens the possibility that they will marry at their own level and increases the possibility that they will marry at higher levels. Two fifths of those who had graduated from college and over half of those who did not get this far married the daughters of laborers. The rest married higher, but only a few of these two groups married daughters of business leaders.

College education seems to have more effect on the sons of white-collar workers than on the sons of laborers in relation to marriage, causing a disproportionate increase in the possibility of the college man in this occupational group marrying up. Of the sons of white-collar workers, those who had college degrees married women from the elite more than any other level (1 out of 5) and twice as much as the sons of this level who had less than college or less than high school. Only 14 per cent of the college graduates married daughters of laborers, compared with 22 per cent for those with less education.

The marriages of the sons of small business men are in many respects similar to those of the sons of white-collar workers, the principal difference being a greater tendency to marry at their own level for both college graduates and those without high school diplomas; fewer college graduates marry into the business elite.

The business leaders who have gone out for higher education marry generally at a higher-status level; those coming from high-status occupational backgrounds tend to marry more at their own status level than the others. It would appear that college education has a paradoxical effect since it increases the likelihood of those of lower occupational backgrounds being accepted as marriage partners by higher-status levels, thus increasing the fluidity of our class structure; but for those already at higher-status levels it tends to increase the rigidity through the tendency to marry at that level.

Although sons of the business elite do not show such extremes in marriage pattern as the sons of laborers, it is clear that education and status combine at this level to play an important role in the choice of mates. Only a small percentage of men born at the top married daughters of laborers, and of these about three fourths have less than a high school diploma. Over a third of the men of this group, when they had college degrees, married at their own level compared with less than a fourth who had less than high school diplomas. When marriages at the high business and professional levels are combined, the differences caused by the education factor become more clear; 58 per cent of the men of this level who had college degrees married women with elite or professional backgrounds compared to only 29 per cent for men who had less than high school diplomas.

For the sons of professional men, those with college education are more likely than those with less education to marry at their own or high business levels, with the exception of high school graduates who have a larger proportion who married into the business elite.

Education seems to have little effect on marriage between farmers and the higher business group, but it does seem to affect marriage with the professional class and others, since only a small percentage of farmers with less than high school education marry daughters of professional men and over three times as many, 20 per cent, of the college educated marry them. Of the sons of farmers who had graduated from college, only a fourth married into their own class compared with twice this proportion among those who had not graduated from high school.

For the possible accumulative effect of generations of one occupational status on the relations between education and marriage, we analyzed each occupational level for all those leaders whose fathers and grandfathers had the same occupation. We can give a few significant conclusions. The grandsons of the elite tend to marry at their own level, no matter what their education; those with college education marry more at the professional level and less at the level of the laboring class than their less-well educated counterparts. The grandsons of professional men are much less likely to marry daughters of laborers or white-collar workers when they have a college education; they are over twice as likely to marry into their own class as the less well educated. For all other classes, those with advanced education marry at a somewhat higher level.

It is now time to turn from the facts of the economic and social origins of the women who marry successful men to the more intimate ones having to do with the kinds of human beings they are and the way they define and play their roles. We will first look at the kinds of roles they assume in the life drama of the mobile man.

7

The Kinds of Women
Who Make Successful Wives

The Role of the Wife

A successful wife may play four major roles, defined in terms of her activities, her interests, and her significance to her husband's career. In one, she limits her interests and activities to being the wife, mother, and manager of the home. In another, she may consider it her principal duty to participate in social and civic activities. Or her greatest importance may be as the helpful, active participant in her husband's job or as consultant to him in his business decisions and the development of his career. Finally, she may devote most of her time and interest to her own profession and career. Occasionally one woman during the course of her life may play all of these roles. More often she assumes but one of two. A woman in the first role may be regarded as acting her part on the family stage—her meaning and defense must be sought in this context; in the second she acts her role in the wider arena of the community; in the third she is the silent or open partner on the job itself; in the last, she is the wife who seeks greater autonomy as a career woman. Let us critically examine each of them.

The family-centered woman knows little or nothing about her husband's job or his business and has only minimal relations with his business associates and their wives. She may have an active social life but within the narrow confines of immediate friends, not related to her husband's job or significant to its practical needs. Such women may be isolated and cut off from close contact with all people outside their immediate families. They may become

120

withdrawn and lonely. What they do, although possibly important to their marital relations, contributes little to the success of their husbands' careers.

Such a role can be vulnerable and dangerous. The experiences of the man as he advances broaden and develop him. As he enters new and larger worlds he meets men and women whom he admires and respects, some of whom may become his friends and his models for status advancement. Their goals, values, and activities become his. His wife meanwhile often remains much what she was when they married and both were people of limited understanding and experience. Her social and personal equipment under these conditions often suffers when he measures her by his newly acquired standards. She may become increasingly isolated while he seeks elsewhere for companionship and intimacy. Divorces sometimes occur; her reveries may be filled unhappily with justified or unjustified suspicions and jealousies. On the other hand, he may be the kind of person who needs and wants "a safe haven," a place where he can relax and be what it is he has always been. Within the limits of such a role, marriages of this kind can be counted rewarding and successful, particularly when the wife is adaptive in developing her behavior within the home to meet the needs of her husband's advancement.

The varieties of this type of family-centered woman include both adequate and inadequate mothers, but in any case their interests are heavily invested in their children. They may act out the role of the mother protestingly and with difficulty or they may do it with ease and, in helping their children, fulfill themselves. Such women may be overinvolved in the lives of their children to the point of domination and rejection of their mates.

In short, these wives, in all their varieties, except for the fact of their marriage to business leaders, are like millions of other women in American culture. Whether the woman is limited or has great capacity for the role she plays, the important questions for us are: How do wives who play this family-centered role relate themselves to their husbands' careers? What happens to the women, to the men, and to their careers? We will answer these questions later by presenting a few cases of successful and unsuccessful wives who play this role.

Within the family the community-centered woman, although a wife and mother, is essentially a hostess to those guests who seem necessary for her husband's advancement. She is also a participant in civic, philanthropic, or social affairs, primarily to advance the family's social position and to help her husband's career. She may play the social game narrowly, within the required limits, by entertaining her husband's business associates; or her activities may range widely to help translate his economic achievement into social advancement, not only for her but for her husband and their children. Obviously, there are many varieties of this type of woman, among them being the woman who ceases to be, or cannot be, the warm person who is a satisfactory wife and creative mother, and the woman who not only transforms her husband's economic success into social achievement for her family but maintains close and rewarding relations with her husband and her children as well as with herself.

A few women, as we said earlier, participate directly in helping their husbands solve their business problems—this, when measured by the career of the husband, being their primary significance. Sometimes they do this by full discussion with him, by comment through understanding his problems, by actual experience on the job itself, or by a basic understanding of business practice and leadership. Such women may or may not be "good wives and mothers"; they may be inadequate hostesses; they may or may not participate in the community.

Finally, there is the professional woman following her own career who may be adequate or inadequate in helping her husband's advancement and as a wife and mother. She may be egocentric to the point that only her own achievement and self-gratification are important to her. In rare cases, however, a woman may be adequate in all the social worlds that the wife of a business man has available. Often in the early part of the career the wife may work to increase their income, perhaps with the hope that her work will develop into a career for herself. Sometimes she resumes such a career after the children are grown or at the death of her husband.

The family-centered woman appears not infrequently, but the wife who is heavily engaged in civic affairs and the social life of the community is most frequent. The wife who is an active and valued consultant in business affairs is rare. The career woman seldom appears. The demands and the needs of the man's career make a separate one for his wife difficult. The necessary changes from place to place as he moves up cannot be accommodated to the advancement of the wife in a separate job, nor is her own professional career easily fitted to that of her husband. Nevertheless, career women—some of them with notable success—are married to business leaders. Often their marriages occur later than those of women who play the other roles and often they take place after one, or both, of them has failed at an earlier marriage. The mobile man may have divorced a wife who was "no longer adequate"— one who had confined herself to the family and had refused, or been unable, to grow. The career woman may have released herself from a husband because of early conflict as their careers were developing.

The personal needs of the husband may be such that the family-centered wife may be most adaptive and, indeed, the only kind some men can tolerate. The single role most likely to be adaptive to the needs of a man's career and to fit most easily the social-class subcultures in which it is placed is the one played on the larger social stage of the community. The combined roles of wife and participant in civic affairs when played well are likely to be supportive to the man and his career.

The Private Worlds of the Wives of Ambitious Men

Given the fact that we are examining a large and important segment of the *lifetime* of most of these men and women of the business elite, perhaps the surest and most revealing way to learn what kinds of women succeed and are effective as the wives of business leaders is to discover how they think and feel about time, their life spans, and how they relate themselves and "their lifetimes" to the past, present, and future. To accomplish this task we have constructed certain idealized models to which the various women fit with varying degrees of accuracy. All of these women who have helped or hindered their husbands' achievement have characteristic feelings about themselves and their relations to time. They relate themselves to the past, present, and future rather differently. Some are fleeing from a past they long to forget and cannot, for they are forever involved with it, feeling the constant backward pull of old unresolved problems. Others may or may not be running away from equally unpleasant social beginnings, yet find no trouble engaging themselves in solving present problems. They have little involvement with the past or the future and concern themselves with the immediate present. Still others get little satisfaction or reward from past or present triumphs in their present participation, for they are seeking something that for them is to be found only in the future. Those who are pulled by the future or engaged with present solving of immediate problems usually fill their roles rather easily.

Those women who look to the past may or may not act easily in their roles and perform successfully. They include several types, for their thoughts about themselves in relation to their past and their varying ways of attachment to it are significantly different. There are women who solve all present problems in terms of unsolved past involvements. Consciously or unconsciously they live in the past and are too attached to it to relate themselves without difficulty to the present or the future. Mobile women who must be constantly learning new ways of thinking, feeling, and acting, and unlearning older ways are thus under grave handicaps. They struggle unceasingly, spending precious psychic and nervous energies fruitlessly to solve yesterday's problems rather than devoting their attention to, and discharging their energies on, the ever-changing world in which they are implicated by their husbands' advancing careers. The learning woman who is easily related to the present or to the future can constantly refresh and strengthen herself by the satisfactions of new experience. Her sister who looks to the past cannot.

There are also those women who are involved with the past in such a way that their present experiences with it reinforce what they now do and give them strength to solve problems concerning future actions. They can look to, and depend upon, the past with positive social results and personal satisfaction, free from unresolved emotional attachments and dilemmas beyond their grasp; however, their attachment is to figures whose power and prestige are symbolically and factually related to them as progenitors, persons with whom they have had satisfactory relations, who as parents and ancestors provide social distinction. Daughters of highborn parents and descendants of such ancestors are psychically and socially benefited—materially as well as technically aided by their inheritance of the learning that was available in this highly valued way of life. Their resources are the social and psychic reinforcements that flow from such social strength and certainty.

However, well-born women may suffer from deep involvements with their families of birth making it difficult for them to play their proper roles in helping their husbands. Casualties, including divorce, suicides, and "social suicides," such as profligate sexual behavior, alcoholism, or marriage to a mate of evil or low reputation, often spring from these sources. Such women find it more difficult to free themselves from their past than do women of lowly birth because it is the custom of their subcultures to look to the past. Their whole significance and that of their social level are founded on their parents and ancestry. Difficult emotional adjustment to parents and ancestors can be "solved" for the mobile persons of low status by rejecting them and running away. Under the socially approved and rewarded ideologies of getting ahead and self-improvement, the basic rejection of their parents often can be disguised and their personal dissatisfactions masked and robed in a pretty costume. But the woman or man born to high status, with parents of distinction and social prestige, cannot follow such a familiar and well-marked path. If the involvement with the family of birth has been satisfactorily reconstructed to meet the needs of maturity there is no need to escape it and even reason to identify one's social self with it.

There is another kind of woman who looks to the past and relates herself to it. This ability is partly a phenomenon of aging. When the leaders and their wives reach, or approach, the age of retirement, many relive the events of the past with deep pleasure and a sense of accomplishment that give them the fortitude to face an ever-changing present. Great emotional involvement with the past at an earlier age would not have been adaptive, but now present joys can be enhanced with an appreciation of the fulfillment of past effort and achievements in present experience. The very role of grandmother when successful is often an expression of this feeling. The wife who has played the role of a family-centered existence, when she becomes a grandmother, may acquire the accumulated honor and respect that often come to such women at this time not only from their children but from their grandchildren.

These several ways of classifying the persons of the wives of business leaders are no more than modal types. But such a conception and estimation of their lifetimes and their involvements with their past, present, and future make it possible to relate their personalities to the roles played by them as mates to their husbands during the changing careers that have made their husbands business leaders. That each woman is much more than the label attached to her as she is related to time is of course obvious. We must now examine each of these five personality types in greater detail: the woman who disregards the past and looks primarily to tomorrow for her fulfillment; she who seeks immediate satisfaction and gives little emphasis to past involvements or to future gains; the woman who mobilizes the prestigeful past to reinforce her present social achievements; the woman who effectively looks to the past and utilizes it to fulfill and strengthen her age status;

and the woman who is involved with the past and finds her present problems and future goals entangled and implicated in its demands and significances.

We can now return to the rather pleasant task of trying to understand Margaret O'Flaherty, wife of John Jacob O'Flaherty, a woman who successfully played her part and helped her husband climb from the bottom and achieve a notable success. Knowledge and insight gained about her necessarily are knowledge and insight about a significant part of his career.

Mrs. O'Flaherty's father made his fortune the hard way. He started first as a laborer, then went to work as a straw boss with the construction company in which his father had spent his life, first with pick and shovel and later, too, as straw boss over a road crew. Big, powerful, and smart, the son worked alongside his father each summer and put himself through school. He graduated as an engineer from a technical college located in a nearby metropolis. He took a job out West helping build a great dam. Soon he came back in the company, first as a superintendent, later as a junior partner and executive vice president, and finally as president of the firm. Under his guidance and drive, competitive firms were bought or ownership and stock arrangements concluded which brought several firms in as small baronies in his empire.

Margaret's father married the daughter of a distinguished San Francisco surgeon shortly after he began his career. He met her through his boss, who sponsored him socially and on the job. Margaret was born a year later, two years before her sister Anne; shortly thereafter the family moved back to New Jersey. The two girls never really experienced the lowly beginnings of their family of birth. But they had known and loved their paternal grandfather, delighted in him as a warm man, while feeling the shelter, comfort, and psychic satisfactions of their own family's position. Nevertheless, they experienced all the excitement and many of the crises of a successful mobile man's career when they moved upward while their father accummulated greater wealth and more and more power and prestige. The mother, a poised lady and the admiring wife of Margaret's and Anne's father, provided a ready model, if sometimes a difficult one, for the growing girls to emulate.

When Margaret married Jake she could love him for being like her grandfather and her father. His lowly beginnings did not frighten or repel her, for she had experienced these in her grandfather, from the security of her own father's economic position and the "social" security learned from her mother. Everyone soon knew that Margaret and Jake were going to have a successful marriage. Subsequent events proved them correct. Part of the answer lies within Margaret's own personality. The resources she commanded were added to Jake's; from them a success story was built. With the aid of depth interviewing and projective psychological studies, let us find out what Margaret is to see how she fashioned her role as Jake's helpmate. We will start by presenting a direct quote from the opening paragraphs of her TAT report:

Mrs. O'Flaherty is able to go right ahead and get what she wants and she knows she can. Mrs. O'Flaherty is quite intelligent. She is not a great organizer by any means because she is not a highly energetic person. Her set in life is more in the direction of letting someone else establish the pace, and operating within that framework. That is, she knows her long-range goals, but the particular method of getting to them she leaves up to the situation.

Margaret O'Flaherty has been able to transfer her own desires for achievement to the career of her husband. She can enjoy today, but she, too, sees life in terms of future "long-range goals." As a part of this we learn:

Although a high-status woman among the wives of mobile men, Mrs. O'Flaherty offers more evidences of mobility drive and abilities than most of them. She is very much aware of her family and her relations with them. She is self-directing—the source of her drive to get ahead, and be self-sufficient, to establish and control her own home is well-internalized and is not a mere reaction to a disliked home situation. She sets her own goals, and makes her own decisions, even in the face of, or perhaps particularly in the face of, parental discouragement.

In view of Mrs. O'Flaherty's marriage, it is interesting to note that she indicates that her family does not approve of her goals, but that she holds up for herself the image of her grandparents. Despite parental discouragement, she is quite able to drive to duplicate her father's family's earlier success, in an independent situation.

This lack of dependence on her family is illustrated at several points in Mrs. O'Flaherty's record. She reveals toward her mother especially a sister-like relationship, one of good feeling basically, with no strong evidence of hostility. However, and this is no doubt of central importance, she does seem to see herself in competition with her mother (and with her sister and other women). This is not to say that she is fighting with her mother openly, or even feels that such a fight is necessary. She does, however, feel that her mother has something, a way of life, a pattern of living, that she herself would like to have. She is strongly aware of the need to dissociate herself from her mother to accomplish a similar goal, and is able to make this break at no great cost to herself. It would not appear to make much difference to Mrs. O'Flaherty at all that her mother might not approve of this.

Another point relevant here is the independence of Mrs. O'Flaherty from other people which enables her to face up to possible disapproval or rejection without undue disturbance. She has a good deal of confidence in her ability to meet situations and accommodate to them. It is also notable that she does not let herself get involved in matters that she does not understand or feels uneasy about. In short, she is a well-controlled woman who gives about as much of herself to people as she wants.

Basically, it would appear that Mrs. O'Flaherty has made a rather difficult-to-achieve adjustment. Her basic male identification as wished-for-son to her father that has caused her to be ambitious and self-controlling has not prevented her from making a positive adjustment to the female role of wife and mother. The wished-for relationship has been, it would appear, successfully transferred to her husband and other males without the hostility to mother or feeling of rejection that might well ensue. In some respects, it might be argued that Mrs. O'Flaherty represents a successful resolution of many of the basic problems and tendencies of the wives of mobile men.

Perhaps it will help to compare her first with her sister Anne, and others like her. Before doing so, we will spend a brief paragraph sketching Anne's development. She, too, grew rather easily into maturity. She accepted her femininity more easily, more quickly resolved her competitive relations with her mother, and from early childhood established warm and close relations with those around her. Her relations with boys were always easy and satisfying. Those who knew them well say that Margaret always assumed responsibility, and that Anne was responsible but enjoyed the immediate present and was likely to have more fun at parties than Margaret. Beautiful and relaxed, Anne was the early recipient of young men's admiration and affection. Being two years younger, she accepted Margaret's directions and during high school the two solved their rivalry. Each had her sphere of competence, and Margaret was always dominant.

Anne, after several engagements, all private and known only to her friends, became engaged to and married James Carter, member of a prominent family in Philadelphia and a powerful leader in American business enterprise.

Clearly, Mrs. O'Flaherty (and other mobile women like her) can look to the future, confident that their rewards are to be found there, rarely fearing it for they are not hampered by psychic involvement with past emotional difficulties. Anne tends to be the woman who seeks immediate satisfaction and is less interested in the demands and rewards of tomorrow. She, too, is free from the emotional ties which would force her to look constantly over her shoulder, fearful of what she might find there. She can be characterized as more sensuous, but her impulse life is expressed within readily approved social forms. She and her kind are more likely to go in for social and fashionable activities of high society when they are available. In this sense she is socially responsible, unlike her sister who is more civic-minded. Margaret believes in helping "organizations build for the future." She takes philanthropy seriously, for her goals and values easily correspond with the activities of such organizations. Her achievement desires are so high that, although today's rewards are satisfactory, only the goals of tomorrow can fully satisfy them. Whatever organizations she enters she is a hard worker within the limits of her energy, con- scientious, and highly responsible. Unlike others of her type she is not the leader, nor is she always willing to take on more and more work.

Although Anne may be in the same civic philanthropies and other worthy enterprises, she is more likely to be there for fun, occasionally for social prestige, because it is the fashionable thing to do, and not for any deeply felt moral responsibility. She enjoys herself in art clubs, social, and fashionable clubs, at sporting events and fashion shows. On the whole, Anne is successful as a social rather than a civic figure. Her house, furniture, pictures, decorations, her clothes tend to express her sensuous pleasure in form, texture, and color. Beauty and good taste, while admired by both, are appreciated rather differently. For Mrs. O'Flaherty, beauty in objects tends to be traditionally defined and significant as such; for Anne the sensuous qualities of beautiful things provide easy channels for sublimated sexuality and pleasure. Since her face and figure permit, and with the help of the beauty salon and her *couturier*, she has followed quite happily her "career of beauty." She tells her daughter that if one cannot be beautiful then "one can be smartly dressed and carefully groomed even without it."

Both Margaret and Anne accumulate jewels and both indulge in conspicuous display, according to their inherited or acquired tastes. Each, in this and other ways, assumes her obligation to transform her husband's economic and occupational position into symbolic objects and activities of high social value, admired by the superior social classes. Thus each helps her husband and her family to assume "their place" in the community. Margaret, the type of woman who looks to the future, accumulates social objects for the house that tend to have "emblematic" significance, investing in solidly conventional things, furniture, art objects, pictures, and rugs, things that mean more socially than they mean in themselves. Anne also accumulates objects that "count," but she is more likely to accent her own taste, support the new arts, and be personally interested in and know the artists.

Anne's relations with males are highly important to her; they are a necessary and simple part of her career. Although her involvement is deep, her relations have always been poised and controlled. She is not afraid of sex. Her relations with her husband are easy and outgoing. She needs male admiration of her beauty, and she believes her husband needs her as something immediately important in his life. Her relations with her husband, since he can respond accordingly, are emotionally satisfying and rewarding. Margaret, less involved in today and more in tomorrow, also finds relations with males, her husband particularly, important and not difficult. But she has a more critical attitude. She does not fear sex but is far less involved and puts lower value upon its fulfillment. She is more inclined than Anne to emphasize its procreative aspects, for she thinks of its consequences. Males are more important in other ways to her. Sex should be played in a low key, for after all with it, as with everything else, one must be responsible.

For Margaret and the woman of tomorrow part of this is connected with the way they view their husbands. The male figure is one of authority but not too difficult to relate to because, although in their way of seeing things they realize that "this is a man's world," they know that women have important and significant parts to play. Furthermore, they are fully aware that some roles they play can often be better than those that are available to men. They can believe "I have my place in the family and the community where I operate. My husband has his, and we share our mutual responsibilities." Finally, successful wives of this type have learned to transfer their own achievement demands to their husbands' careers.

The woman of today, such as Anne, looks at her husband in somewhat the same way, but she views herself more as a sexual object, and she sees her husband as valuing her more because she is. She believes she is socially active and does her share partly because she wants to make life pleasant and fun for him. This includes her choice of clothes, the kinds of parties she gives and attends, and the games in which they participate or attend as spectators. She tells her intimates not only that a woman's position is interesting and satisfactory but that, for a woman who knows how, it is subtle and provides deep satisfactions. She is highly conscious of her female self, for life itself to her is founded on the basic sexual division. Accordingly there must be a division of responsibility between men and women. "What a woman is, a man can't be, and isn't that wonderful for us?"

Being a part of the woman's world as distinct from the man's does not frighten Margaret either. Knowing it is a man's world, she can stay in her own or enter the other without grave anxiety. Margaret easily accepts the necessity of the division of labor between her and Jake, for she knows that such a relation properly conducted is highly rewarding. Given more energy and more competitive spirit, such a woman can easily become the silent partner or active participant in her husband's affairs. Nor would she be involved deeply in conflict over the necessity at times of leaving the wife's role to enter her own career. Some, when they choose such a course, can still value the role of wife and mother. Others cannot, their marriages being filled with tension or ending in divorce. Margaret and her kind are not much involved in the career versus wife problem which concerns so many American women. On the contrary, they can deeply value their roles as women, feeling that the most advantageous and safest place to play this role is as the wife of an admiring and devoted husband. When such women get into difficulties within this sphere it is more often not so much because of their own incapacity as because of a husband who is unable to play his part or because larger events disturb the husband-wife relation.

The woman who thinks of today in terms of future consequences is likely to have a realistic picture of the world. She is likely to have not only an intelligent but also a moral interest. She has little trouble with herself in relating to problems of the family and to her husband's needs and problems. Anne (and her kind) understands more "instinctively" than analytically, sometimes availing herself of the easy rubrics of convention and fashion, but more often using the sure perceptions of her basic training.

Mobile women of either type from lower levels easily find

worthy and exciting models to emulate. They have no trouble in imitating the women of superior status about them. When younger, each can easily accept the guidance of a social arbiter. Each, particularly the woman involved with the future, can carry out the directions of such people and assume some of the social labor of older women to whom they look for approval and from whom they continually learn. Women, gaining their satisfactions more from today, of course, choose different models. At a social function they are more likely to "grace a social gathering to make the men feel the party was a success."

As we know from analyzing Margaret O'Flaherty and those like her, the woman who looks to the future is more likely than the woman who lives for today to have been rivalrous with her mother. Anne, like other women deriving the meaning of the world from today, easily transferred her affections from her parents. They have little or no trouble in sexual competition with older women. Anne is mildly flirtatious but not competitive with other wives when husbands are about. In general, she knows (as does Margaret) how to keep her competitive feelings well in hand and not allow them to interfere with an easy relationship to women of her own age. Women tend to like and trust her, particularly women of her own kind.

Both types of women, confident in their husbands' ability to solve problems, enjoy strong psychic and social rewards from their achievements. Each is able to strengthen her husband when he fears failure. Anne not only comforts her husband when he needs it but is more likely to distract him at such times by emotional and physical gratifications. Margaret is aware of the need to conserve her husband's energies and to reduce and organize his social engagements to fit his needs. Anne is less aware of the limits of her husband's energy output. She is too likely to rely on pleasure and fun to allow her husband to forget his troubles by relaxing. Each has the ability to transfer her desire to be a male and compete in a male world to her aspirations for her husband's success.

Both these women believe in and practice good form and prize ordered relations, but to Margaret and the woman of tomorrow codes are more important, and the older social rituals are to be either respected or argued down as rationally inconsequential. Anne places more emphasis on casual interpersonal relations, tends to be more exploratory, but still prizes an ordered manner of relating herself to people.

Each of these women can operate easily in and out of her family. Each may be criticized, but it does not prevent her from venturing into the activities which interest her. Each highly values her husband and his career but, although her present position depends on him, she often has a strong belief in her ability to stand on her own. When fears are present they are not so overpowering that it is impossible to participate in the immediate world around her. However, the woman of today, dependent on her beauty for her success, when approaching middle age often fears its loss and the consequent adjustment.

In this general discussion of Anne and Margaret, we have related each to her type more than to the individual variations, our interest being more in the kinds of women who are wives of successful leaders than in the individual woman.

Both are illustrations of ideal types, modalities around which the personal characteristics of many other successful wives of business men cluster. Some women possess some of these characteristics but not others. On the whole, their characteristics have been stated with emphasis on those most likely to produce positive effects on the career of the business leader. A clear demarcation cannot always be made for all women for the several personality types.

The woman who looks to the past and who is forever involved with its unresolved problems while she attempts to solve present ones does not often appear in our small sample. Her comparative absence may be significant. It seems improbable that she would be present in any large numbers, for she is ill equipped to maintain herself in the present and face the future in the career of her husband. Furthermore, it is not likely that she could easily relate

herself to most of the highly ambitious driving men who are constantly changing their life situations and continually learning
what has to be known to live in the new environments they invade.
Such men too often frighten and repel women of this kind rather
than attract and give them a sense of security.

Contemporary Cinderellas, born to lowly status, filled with
anxiety, and limited to a vision derived from such position, are not
likely to be bold enough to drive in state to the high places. Such
a ride is more than their personalities can bear. Nor are they
likely to welcome the prince who comes to fetch them. Such
women are unlikely to marry the hard-driving mobile men and
climb the hazardous and at times perilous path to the stars. Nor
could they, except in fantasy, marry the boss's son and exist as
frightened strangers in an alien land far distant from that of their
nativity. Sometimes they do, but their adjustments to their new
worlds and their marriages are likely to be difficult and carried on
under emotional stress.

We will examine the lives of three women, who rose with their
husbands from lower ranks, each of whom assumed the role of the
wife and mother and centered her life within the family. This role
is one in which each type of personality can make a satisfactory
adjustment. Even the woman who looks to the past may find a
place where she can continue being with her husband. By sharpen-
ing our focus and limiting our observations to the role of the
family-centered wife we can examine the successful and unsuccessful adjustments and study some of the different kinds of personalities which play this role. Let us first examine the private
world of Mrs. Karl Openhauser.

The Personalities of Three Wives of American Executives

Mrs. Karl Openhauser is the wife of the vice president of a large
utilities corporation. Her husband rose rapidly by working and
putting himself through college and postgraduate work in engineering. Mrs. Openhauser did not go to college. She was a beautiful

young woman, bright, active, and one of several children. Her parents came from Germany, as did her husband's. The Openhausers now live in a solid, respectable neighborhood in Milwaukee. They first met in high school. The father of each was a semi-skilled laborer. Mr. Openhauser has just turned fifty; his wife is several years his junior.

Most of Mrs. Openhauser's limited energies are spent in her home. She suffers from a number of ailments and has had two serious operations. With these brief observations, let us turn to the inner world of Mrs. Openhauser.

Mrs. Openhauser seems to be a person who has never recovered from the shock that leaving her parents to marry represented to her. She appears now in middle age to be a depressed and frightened woman, a person who feels that her life has been misspent, that she might have been a much more pleasing and happier person had she not been confronted with the enormous and difficult tasks of adulthood. There is a strong suggestion that her father was primarily interested in his sons and that Mrs. Openhauser would like to fill the role of son for the father. She was not able finally to resolve the conflict between the desire to leave the isolation and rejection of the home and the desire to remain and prove to herself that she really was loved and wanted and not rejected. There are two concomitants of this conflict. In the first place, Mrs. Openhauser is basically oriented to the past, to regrets, to reevaluations of decisions, and to "I-told-you-so's." Second, she is constantly on the alert for evidences of persons' leaving her; she tends to see herself as guilty for their leaving.

Mrs. Openhauser is indecisive. She is ready to blame others, and to express negative feelings in a quick, uncensored reaction to problems. This burst of feeling is quickly stifled, however, in a wave of self-repudiation and abnegation, in which she takes unto herself the blame and guilt. One of the results, and a fairly apparent one, is the habit of making tasks difficult for herself. Recalling her physical complaints, we realize that her inability to express negative feelings, her bottling them up, along with the fatigue resulting from this, underlie or aggravate the many physical problems she has encountered.

"It is not likely that Mrs. Openhauser would have interest in, or energy for, participation beyond the family circle. It is probable," the report on her personality continues, "that wider social participation represents too great a threat in terms of rejection, real or potential, for her to be able to sustain friendly but non-intimate relationships. She will get too tired and find the strain too great for much of this kind of wider participation."

Mrs. Openhauser has stayed within the family circle, partly protected by her chronic illness from the social and psychological threats of the new social world into which she was propelled by her husband's rise. Meanwhile, in reverie and emotion she is still held to past commitments.

There is little need to discuss the unhappy adjustment Mrs. Openhauser has made as a frightened woman looking nostalgically back to a protected girlhood. Her role as a sick wife cut off from her husband's career now protects her from the hazards created by his career advancements.

The present Mrs. Carleton (the second of the three family-centered wives) met her husband immediately after she had quit high school near the end of her junior year. She was then seventeen. She was of Slavic stock, her father the son of an immigrant. He had moved west and located in a large city on the Pacific Coast to spend his life in a semi-skilled job in a cement plant. Katy was the fifth of six children. When John Carleton first saw her she was a "car-hop" serving him a sandwich in a drive-in restaurant. Katy was tall, blonde, young, and beautiful. Following several such meetings she accepted invitations to go dancing and bowling; a few months later they were engaged to be married.

When John married her he was an underpaid clerk in a large office. They moved to a small apartment and began their climb to their present high position. He went to night school and studied finance and salesmanship to supplement his high school training. His work was appreciated by his superiors, for he had enormous drive and great capacity for hard work, particularly in learning what to do in new jobs which were always those just above him. He was early marked for promotion and rose rapidly. Sometimes this was done with ruthless disregard for the well-being of anyone other than himself. Meanwhile Katy became the mother of two sons and later a daughter. After the first child they moved to a two-family house in a better neighborhood and, as each child was born, they told themselves that they needed more space and a better place for their children. Each time they moved to a larger house and a better neighborhood. Meanwhile Carleton went from the lower levels of management to the executive vice presidency of an important and powerful corporation.

They now live in a solid, middle-class suburb. It is a neighborhood, however, where none of the families of the top executives of his own or other organizations such as his live. It is respectable, well above average, but not socially distinguished. Katy knows few of her neighbors. The children make their own friends among their high school classmates, the sons and daughters of families within the neighborhood. Katy and her children rarely see Mr. Carleton. He is seldom home for dinner and more often than not is absent on weekends. Mrs. Carleton says, "John is the most ambitious man I ever knew. He drives and drives all of the time." Then she adds that she wishes that John could be home for dinner with her just once a week—"it would be like old times."

When we asked John Carleton for a home interview, as we did with all the men studied, he replied, "Couldn't it be somewhere else instead, such as the club?"

"Isn't your wife part of the story?"

"Definitely not. I believe she would agree with me that the only way she has helped is by doing a good job of raising our three children so that I don't have to take time out to straighten out a bunch of brats, and by doing a minimum of griping because I am home so little. I spend on the average of one dinner home a week. So I'd prefer the club for this interview, if at all possible.

"I've kept my home life completely separate from business

always. My wife has never met my business associates' wives, and never will, if I can help it! I get a salary almost as much as Eisenhower and she can't even imagine half that!"

Meanwhile, Katy retains much of her beauty and is still the faithful wife and good mother. Those who have seen her and had the opportunity to talk her life over with her believe that on the whole Katy is not discontented with herself or her world. Given these facts, one wonders what she is like as a person, why it is possible for her to make this seemingly satisfactory (to her) adjustment.

Reports on the psychological tests provide insight into the private world that allows her to play the role she has. Given her social background and her personality it seems likely she could not have played any other and remained Mr. Carleton's wife. Furthermore, it seems probable that few other types of persons could have played her role. Also, it is probable that much of what she is and what she does provides Mr. Carleton with considerable satisfaction and allows him to continue being what he is.

Katy Carleton [we are informed] is a passive, accepting person with very few personal resources to fall back on. She is highly dependent upon others to give her life meaning and to shape her goals. Although a friendly person she is without ability to organize or intrude herself socially. She easily accepts males on their terms, sees them as strong, controlling, and dominating. Her emotional adjustments to them are passive. She does resent, however, the strong ambitions and exhibitionism in which she sees males participate. Her early background does not appear to any great extent in her fantasy life. Her father not at all. There is little evidence of hostility to her mother. Her separation from her parents is rather complete. She has always been on her own and dependent upon her limited resources for most of her experience. In general, it seems that when she grew up she had little involvement with anyone or anything in her life. She is not involved with her past. In the absence of the direction provided by husband or home she may become fatigued and relatively inactive.

Nevertheless, she is a rather cheerful person who takes things pretty much as they come without letting herself become too upset about problems or people. She does not herself have ambitions. She feels that someone will inform her of what to do, where to go, and is ordinarily quite willing to go along. Since her marriage, her husband has provided this direction.

One of the most notable features of her personality is her lack of anxiety. Mrs. Carleton is not a frightened person nor a tense one. She has no need to punish people. She is quite willing to accept the fact that she may not always be desirable to others, including her husband, but she does believe that by quietly presenting her case and by going on day by day pretty much as she has, she will carry the day in the face of rejection. She is understanding of her children and offers comfort and control whenever they need them. While quickly responsive to other people, she has little insight into their more basic motivations.

Mrs. Carleton, with a past that does not intrude itself on her present, with little anxiety, and with no ordered ambitions for herself, is as easy with others as she is with herself. She is involved with the present, not the past or the future. Her passive nature and her weak emotional needs equip her to take what for others would be risks. She can do this because there are no pursuers from within forcing her to make demands on a husband unwilling and unable to meet them. The world is not threatening to her, nor is she ridden by anxiety as are many women who grew up in her early environment and never made peace with it, with their parents, or with themselves. Anxious women who make these demands tend to live out their lives in the social world of their origin.

But it would be claiming too much to insist that Katy's life is wholly satisfying to her or to her husband. He himself has declared, when speaking of his inordinate desire to climb to still greater heights, that "it would be nice if Katy knew what to do to help." The combination of her social background, which meagerly equipped her for full partnership in a success story, her own dependent and passive personality—perhaps these coupled with her husband's unconscious efforts to isolate her from his world, to keep her home in a safe place to which he can retreat—have made it impossible for her to be anything more than she is. As the house-wife who rears the children and keeps the house in order, she is an adequate wife and mother. But she is little more. She is not directly assisting Mr. Carleton to translate his economic success into high social achievement or aiding her husband to improve his chances for still greater success. Judged crassly on the basis of economic and social advancement, neither the role Mrs. Carleton plays nor her way of playing it is fully satisfactory either to her husband, to herself, or to the kind of career he has developed. Judged by other standards, perhaps her way of solving her problems is more than adequate.

We need only briefly relate the story of Mrs. Emil Fredericks. She is not entangled with the past; tomorrow absorbs most of her thoughts and energies. She accepts life easily. She has found no difficulty in relating her emotional development at an earlier period to her mother, father, and brothers and, later, her husband and children.

She and Mr. Fredericks are second-generation American. They started at the bottom with no formal education. He has now advanced to the vice presidency of a large international corporation. Mrs. Fredericks has always remained the housewife and good mother, but through the use of many instrumentalities of "self-improvement" she has "kept up." She knows and consults Emily Post. She has used other outside authoritative functionaries to help her: interior decorators, an architect, a charm school, and special courses on proper ways to cook, play bridge, dance, and carry on social activities within the limited range of her neighborhood friends. She has taken courses in correct English and for years has belonged to the book clubs. Through self-improvement the Fredericks have advanced together, each performing his or her assigned task in mutual aid. They learn as they go, each in his own sphere. She stays at home and looks out for the children. They entertain neighborhood friends in a middle-class suburb. Although pleased with their progress they are still ambitious; increasingly this has become an ambition for their children who are now in college. Their friends count them both very successful people.

The business man's wife who plays the family-centered role may find it satisfying for herself and those whom she loves and whose lives are dependent on her; or she may be unsuccessful, unhappy, and fail to contribute to the happiness or success of her husband. Those mobile women who are presently oriented or who are concerned with the future and not with the past are most likely to fit the role. Given the nature of the changing lives they lead and the kinds of men they marry, this would be expected. However, not all women who look to the past and are involved with it are poorly adjusted. We will examine the lives of some of them in Chapter VIII which discusses the top families.

The variety of wives of business leaders is more numerous than the diversity of personality among their husbands. The men necessarily must make satisfactory adjustments to a competitive world, to their business and public lives, or face being eliminated. Each executive knows of such men, some more able than himself, who were unable to adjust their inner lives satisfactorily to the exacting demands of mobility (or did not want to), who quit, were fired, or, as some of them say, "quietly plateaued off"—stayed where they were and stopped all struggle to advance. Mobility for each ended. The wives of ambitious leaders, not necessarily facing the daily demands of the job and having a variety of roles present and possible, can tolerate the vicissitudes more easily. The poorly prepared, the incapable, as well as the well-adjusted, highly autonomous women, can choose roles that fit their needs and play them more according to inner than to outward demands. It seems probable, given the diversity of social and economic backgrounds, family training and early experience, that they vary as widely in personality as most groups of American women.

8

The Public and Private
Worlds of the Birth Elite

Ten Generations

The lives and careers of mobile leaders have been examined in previous chapters. In this we shall study the private and public worlds of the birth elite. Because the place of the family is of primary importance in understanding business leaders of this kind we shall pay particular attention to the relations of fathers and sons, husbands and wives, and other family members. The problems of men born to an "old" elite, three or more generations at the top, are different from those of the "recent" elite, those born to fathers who were the first generation to occupy this position; therefore, we shall analyze both types. We shall also learn what we can about how and in what way their families influence occupational succession in American big business. Alton Dobson and his wife are excellent examples of the old elite. We will begin our inquiry by learning what kind of people they are and what part the family played in the career of this representative of the men who were born to position.

Alton Dobson's great-grandfather and his father's father before him were recognized as important figures in the business world. Socially the Dobson family has been prominent in New England for many generations. Since one fourth of the business leaders are sons of big business men and only one eighth are grandsons, Dobson represents a small but important group. They, their careers, their families, and their social worlds contrast sharply with the world of mobile men. Dobson, throughout his life, has

144

stayed in the *social* position given him by birth. The security of birth and family is of the utmost importance to him and his position.

Seemingly all men born to business leaders share a common position. Occupationally this is largely true, but socially it is not. The recent elite, the leaders who are sons of mobile men, are not in families with firmly established and consolidated positions; their family's place in the community is very different from that of the older families like the Dobsons. The new and old birth elites have different problems to solve—one is insecure socially, and the other firmly placed and secure.

We first see Alton Dobson through the eyes of the man who interviewed him.

"When I went into Alton Dobson's office," the interviewer wrote, "I felt a little let down. The quarters were almost cramped; his desk was a roll top. There were indications of today's efficiency, yet all of it said that many men, generations before Alton Dobson, had ruled from these modest quarters and that he, the present occupant, would pass his empire on to a proper aspirant of the next generation, well trained to take command. His secretary, an elderly, spinsterish person, might have been a character in a Howells novel out of nineteenth-century Boston. Later when I saw the Beacon Street house I found its exterior somewhat dull and much like all of them on that street. But the interior was something else. It, too, was from the past. Despite some of the intrusive Victorian furniture, most of it went back to the classical elegance of the Georgian period. The house was quiet; it had the stillness and unmoving quality of the past about it. A butler took me to the library where Alton Dobson was sipping a brandy with his after dinner coffee. He looked small and insignificant against the background of the high walls, filled with tier upon tier of beautifully bound books.

"He told me of his family. Some time before the Revolution they started in the fishing trade, built ships and sent them to the West Indies, to Africa and China. This branch of the family gradually gave up shipbuilding and trade. From their financial knowledge gained as 'merchant princes' they moved into banking and soon owned one of the most powerful banks in the Eastern United States. Now the stock is well distributed, but the Dobson name and the bank as an institution are often synonymous. He went to St. Mark's, to Harvard, 'got no more than a gentleman's C,' was coxswain on the crew (very proud of this), a member of a final club, spent a year abroad, another at the Harvard Law School, and then started as a clerk in another bank to learn the business. He learned to his astonishment that his business colleagues thought him a good business man and before long he was an employee 'of the bank my family has been associated with for so long, and after serving my time at the small desks I was promoted to a higher place and in time the bank made me president. The family name didn't hurt, but I know if I had not possessed ability I would never have been allowed to reach any position of importance in this bank. Perhaps I shouldn't say this. I know it's immodest, but to make my point—one of my cousins tried to do much what I've done. He just didn't have it. Finally, even he knew it, maybe because he got no place. He quit and is now living very modestly on a small inheritance in the South of France.'

"Outwardly he fitted the conventional role of the conservative bank president and the inheritor of social status well established by many generations of Dobsons. I was not prepared for his responses to the personality tests. They revealed something quite different.

"When he looked at the card of the athletic man on the rope, I expected the usual traditional and conventional answers, such as the man was a trapeze performer and, after prodding, to hear he was going up or coming down the rope. Mr. Dobson looked at the card, took his glasses off his nose, and turned to me with a big smile and a knowing look: 'That fellow on the rope is evidently escaping from some place. Might be a fire although it's more apt to be—I could tell you something, but I wouldn't want you to put it down. He might have just heard the lady's husband come in the door. He's thrown his clothes out the window, and he's making a hasty descent out the fire escape. That would account for his being in the nude.'

"I was amused. I learned that Mr. Dobson was not the only one of his social class who seemed to have an inner freedom and an easy way of dealing with his 'impulse life.' True they are conventional in manner, their business roles are exemplary, and their moral behavior without reproach, but some of them find joy in life and are capable of having fun.

"While we were having a drink before I left, the conversation turned to his civic and social life and the kinds of clubs and organizations to which he and his wife belonged. I told him I'd like to know what they were and how he felt about them. He sighed:

" 'I must belong to hundreds of associations. I'm constantly trying to weed them out. I've taken a pretty active part in some; sometimes I spread myself too thin. I belong to the National and State Chambers of Commerce, the NAM, American Banking Institute, and to the Harvard and Racquet Clubs. I belong to certain social clubs—you don't join one, you're born to it. I belong to some others but they don't amount to anything.' What philanthropic and public service organizations? He smiled. 'Do you really want them? Here are some that I'm active in. Mother and Infant Welfare Society, the Historical Society, the Geographic Society; I used to be on the board of directors of the national Polio organization. I am on the board of the Art Museum; I'm on the boards of two prep schools. They take about as much time as my other extracurricular activities. The Historical Society is a closely knit organization tied up with New England. We publish our own histories. My mother was on the board of the Mother and Infant Welfare Society for some twenty-odd years. She got off and they wanted me to come on.' Are you also interested in these groups? 'Oh, yes, I wouldn't be an officer unless I were interested. I've turned down many things that I thought would be nice but I'm not personally interested in them or they have nothing to do with the company.'

"Political organizations? 'I've done very little in politics. That's just because I haven't taken the time, or I'm not a good enough citizen. But I contribute. I've voted the Republican ticket every time except in some local cases where I split my ticket.'

" 'My friends? Basically, my good friends are from St. Mark's. My contact with them now is mostly social. A few friends are from college. Most of my friends are business executives, pretty much so. Loads of them turn out to be clients or lawyers, bankers —in that category. I'm not society minded at all, only my wife is. I'm usually involved in extracurricular activities so much that I don't gad about.

" 'My wife entertains our social and business friends. She takes an active part; she has to. She doesn't go on business trips, but she's active here. She wouldn't see me if she weren't. We entertain a lot at home.' "

Mr. Dobson and those who belong to the older birth elite participate in the community differently from those recently arrived. The birth elite are active in a greater variety of philanthropic and civic organizations and social clubs. Many of the outstanding and more prestigeful social clubs are not open to the newly arrived elite or to those whose fathers were the first to climb from social obscurity. Mr. Dobson had learned this at St. Mark's and Harvard; others of his kind grew up with such knowledge or gained it before going to Yale, Princeton, and other undergraduate, socially distinguished colleges. But mobile young men, striving to reach high position at such places, always learn sooner or later, as had Jake O'Flaherty, that "people like us are okay to know and be friends with, but it takes a great-great-grandfather to get you in the better clubs of Boston or New York." Mr. Dobson, while speaking of his undergraduate class, said he had known young Franklin Roosevelt and that, despite the fact that their families saw each other and were distantly related, he had "never liked Frank, too damned unreliable and egocentric. Had Jim Farley and Jake O'Flaherty asked me I could have told them. But then Mrs. Dobson and I never knew either of them or their wives well enough to tell them when it might have done some good. As Mrs. Dobson will tell you, the Coolidges were nobodies socially, but old Cal was the best President this country's had since Lincoln."

Mrs. Alton Dobson: Custodian of a Lineage

Throughout her adult life Mrs. Alton Dobson has counted on, and effectively used, the prestige and power of her birth into an old family of inherited wealth and standing. In the last few years she has become a most respected older woman whose authoritative position in the community's civic and social life is constantly being strengthened by her role as the social arbiter whose very presence refers to the great days of the past "when society meant something." She speaks for it and on most occasions her word is law.

At home she is grandmother to her eight grandchildren. Three granddaughters were almost openly proud of her presence at their coming-out parties. They indulge her and she them, giving advice about young men which their parents sometimes consider "almost scandalous" and telling tales of childhood indiscretions of their own parents. She and her husband have arrived at that age when their early achievements are now embodied within their persons so that their children, with sons and daughters of their own and no longer rebellious against parental control, take pride and delight in their parents. Given the values and standards of their level, their own security is partly dependent on the present re-creation of the past to make it significant and relevant for present and future undertakings. Mrs. Dobson's children, about to become the older generation, need to know and become the repositories of the traditional lore of their families; such understanding and its resultant prestigeful significance are meaningful parts of their inheritance.

Mrs. Dobson's successful use of the past clearly includes the prestige of her family as well as the enhancement of her personal prestige because of her increased age. Many of the things she does now which involve references to, and use of, the past and are rewarding would not have been possible when she was younger. Women from other levels of society, at or below the elite, may also achieve her power to use the past, but those of lesser social and occupational stature necessarily must use it differently.

Mrs. Dobson [the TAT report says] is a pleasant-mannered, rather quiet woman who is quite conscious of her age and feels she is ready to assume a role of adviser and commentator on the passing scene, rather than participate actively in the turmoil that surrounds her. She is not too closely involved with her husband, and has worked out to her own satisfaction an accepting role with him, where she plays little part in his wider activities.

She is rather chatty, and flighty, in her first approach to situations, talking about her superficial associations. She dwells on genealogy, on mutual friends and associates, on the history or location of places. The process has the considerable advantage of permitting her to determine whether or not she will find it safe to become more deeply involved with the situation, or whether she should withdraw and remain at some distance, safe in the history of past things.

This kind of approach to people and problems is no doubt the result of, and is consistent with, her girlhood experiences of being overwhelmed, inundated, by feelings and emotions to the extent of loss of self-control. Thus there is a backdrop of black, violent storms, of unchecked threat, which emerges only at a few points. This is quite consistent with her usual style of organizing the world; the chatty manner and hesitant approach give her time to prepare herself against this hidden threat.

In common with several of this high-status group of women, Mrs. Dobson has a marked tendency to identify persons in terms of their background—family or spatial—and to want to know who people are before she begins to concern herself with them. This is not an instance of hostility, however. By and large, Mrs. Dobson is friendly, assumes that people are going to be pleasant and interesting, and that what she says about herself and past events will interest people.

Those women born to the first generation of the birth elite and those who rose to it in their own lifetimes face different problems when using past times for present purposes. The pride of the man and woman who rose from the bottom to the top, while pervasive in America, is not always shared by their children. The man and his wife still carrying the marks of their beginnings may themselves prefer to forget the past and find difficulty relating to it. Sometimes their habit of thinking of today only in terms of tomorrow prevents them. Their children, born to and trained in another subculture and experiencing different class values from those of their parents, also may be willing to accept their parents only in terms of the present. The past is dead for both of them. In effect, mobile men and their wives often train their children to live in another world and separate themselves from what the parents are. Sometimes this separation results in tragedy for both generations. The "crude" father and socially unequipped mother, their achievements forgotten, find themselves rejected. Their children sometimes feel restless, alone, and without social foundations on which to build solid lives. Many personal and social disabilities may result, including marital unhappiness, an emotional instability that makes realistic adjustment difficult or impossible, and other personal disorders. The sons of mobile men often feel that the great shadow of the father denies them the warmth necessary for self-development. Many sons and daughters of such men and women, of course, probably the majority, work out their own solutions, often with the insightful help of their parents.

Children born to any occupational or social level may or may not be capable of using their past experience satisfactorily. The sons and daughters of the birth elite of many generations, as is well known, have their difficulties. Some fail miserably; many are the chronic patients of society psychiatrists. The children of the newly successful father have their own troubles growing up, as do those of the old families, their troubles often springing from different sources; but, since such a large percentage of both are able to compete successfully in the increasingly competitive world of Big Business, it is certain that most of them solve the problems of maturation and adjust realistically and favorably to the complexities of modern life.

The wives of the birth elite, like those who entered it through their and their husbands' achievement, play all four roles of wife, community leader, business adviser, and career woman. Their personal outlooks may adhere to the past to the point that adjustment is not possible, or they may be oriented to the future, or involved with the present. Furthermore, such women may use the past positively and successfully for their adjustments and, as life continues, do this more successfully and with greater benefit to themselves as they advance in years.

The family plays a dominant and important part in who gets to the top and who stays there. The wife and mother is the crucial person in the early and probably the later development of the child. Around her many of the emotional problems and their resolution are centered. Through her much of the core of our culture flows into the persons and habitual responses of each new generation. The rise of many successful men and the achievements of those born to the elite are often directly related to the influence of their mothers. Most of them are consciously aware of the powerful influence of their mothers. Most say they are more like their mothers than their fathers, and that their mothers had more to do with firing them with ambition or "beating it into me" than did their fathers. Increasingly the family, particularly the roles and persons of the wife and the mother, must be understood in the study of occupational succession. From them the old and new generations are psychically formed and developed, and out of them the future leaders of the great business enterprises socially emerge.

Civic and Social Life of the Two Elites

Mr. Ralph Danvers' account of his participation in the civic and social life of his community is in sharp contrast with Alton Dobson's. Mr. Danvers is a mobile man who has had great success in business. He is civic-minded and personally interested in worthy philanthropies and more than willing to spend his energies and skill for the welfare of his community.

Mr. Danvers enjoyed talking about his career to the interviewer but spent most of his time discussing his activities with the Catholic Boys' Club, his major interest. His career with the Boys' Club—and it is a career—started some time back. He was invited to sit in on the local board meetings and then later was asked to become a member of the board. Soon he was given chairmanship of the fund-raising committee, and more money was raised than in previous years. After that he kept getting more prominent positions.

His success in this work is apparently connected with the time he has devoted to the jobs assigned to him and his use of novel devices and ideas, often from the merchandising field. As he reviewed the way he had approached every new position held in the club, he recalled that every time he was told, " 'Ralph, you'll never do it, Ralph you're crazy!' why it worked every time! Now the others doing the same type of work wouldn't think of doing it any other way."

"It was evident," the interviewer said, "that he was impressed—and probably tried to impress me—with the 'big names' of the other men on the committees; with every anecdote he gave me a 'list' of the other members of the committee, who they were, what they did, how many were millionaires, and with a laugh said, 'They have ten times as much money as I have.' He would first give their names, and then, as if to make sure I knew whom he was talking about, he would give their full names; often, he would comment that they were very good friends of his and what association he had with them. Oddly enough, I did not have the impression that he was bragging; he talked about it in a way that made me feel that he was a very mobile man, that what he said was true, and that it sort of fitted him, i.e., his general excitement and enthusiasm. It was also very obvious that he enjoyed telling me these stories.

"At present, he is attempting to raise funds for the rejuvenation of one of the slum area clubs. A friend 'happened' to bring him down there, i.e., he was apparently brought with the hope that he would get particularly interested in it—and when he saw the miserable condition that it was in, he decided to do something about it. He said that just because it is primarily Negro does not mean that the organization can neglect it; 'in fact,' he added, 'it is in precisely those neighborhoods that the most work is needed.' "

Mr. Danvers' view of his participation in civic affairs is different from Mr. Dobson's. His way of acting and his memberships are also different. Mr. Danvers belongs to few organizations and concentrates on one. His energies are still being expanded in his business mobility. He sees civic organizations as a means to do important things and meet important people. Mr. Dobson more often sees them and the values they embody as ends in themselves, or else he invests his energies in them because of "family inheritance." Many have been thrust upon him. He belongs to more than he feels he can properly serve. They are rarely instruments for his own advancement, nor are they organizations which he knows his company wants him to assist as his share of its public relations program. Generally, but not always, mobile men and women enter and use philanthropic and civic organizations "to know and be known by" the right people. Often they are *instruments* of social mobility and *means* by which people of talent, energy, and drive can advance themselves. Sometimes this mobility function is coordinated with their own deep moral convictions.

Occasionally the woman who plays the community role spends her time in church and associations interested in ethical goals, disregarding the functional needs of her role for the advancement of her husband and family. The choices of civic organizations by the mobile woman and her husband, more often than not, are not crassly exploitative nor consciously thought-out stratagems of the social climber, but simply adaptations of what they think are proper and right things to do. Often they are the activities which the mobile woman sees others of her kind engaged in, activities supported by women she admires. Usually she is welcomed as an ally while still being watched as a competitor. Margaret O'Flaherty, mobile, although born to a father of high position, not being hostile or overtly aggressive, fits into such organizations easily. She is always the follower who makes suggestions to the boards of her philanthropies without demanding that they must be followed.

Ordinarily the older birth elite belongs to a greater variety of associations, civic and social, than do the mobile elite, particularly those of the latter group who have settled for a middle-class status. Although the middle class are joiners, as individuals they tend to belong to fewer organizations than the birth elite. The activities of the associations to which the elite belong are in many respects distinctly different from those of the middle levels. Associations engaged in sacred or semi-sacred rituals and practices rarely concern the elite. The white-collar and working levels are many times more concerned with activities involving sacred rituals than the elite, who are, for example, rarely interested in secret societies and lodges.[1] In general the use of symbols which directly arouse the emotions, although favored by the lower levels, are shunned by the mobile and birth elites. The elite, when involved with emotional symbols such as those in philanthropic and civic associations, tend to stress the operation and manipulation of them as instrumental activities necessary for putting their beliefs and values into practical action. The evocative symbol of the motherless child is meaningful to them, but the association is likely to use it to advance a program of adoption; the symbols of maternity and motherhood are significant but more in terms of philanthropies to arouse public emotion to help worthy enterprises.

The mobile and birth elites share a common sense of belonging to the higher levels of their occupations. Most of them feel, if they do not explicitly recognize, that they are socially above the ordinary people about them, this being more often true of the wives and still more true of those with marriageable offspring. Within these levels there are recognizable gradations. The old birth elite clearly participate in a way of life that tends to set them off from the more recently arrived. Among the mobile

[1] W. Lloyd Warner, *American Life: Dream and Reality* (Chicago: The University of Chicago Press, 1953), ch. IX, "Associations in America," pp. 191-209.

families there are also gradations. Sometimes the regions they live in are expressive of the differences among them; sometimes it is the prestige and power of their social organizations; at other times the family name itself is sufficient. A check on the social registers showed that less than half of the elite were members, indicating that it takes time for those who come from the lower ranks to receive social recognition for their economic and occupational accomplishments. Part of this lapse in time is accounted for by the difficulty in learning to want such recognition, in learning how to do the "right things," getting to know the right people and, above all, arriving at a place where the right people, those who have arrived before, accept them as social equals. Franklin Roosevelt's father expressed his individual feelings and values by refusing to become involved with the Vanderbilt parvenus, but he expressed them as a member of his class. Even his son, notably liberal and a friend of the common man, approved of his father's behavior.

Not only are occupational accomplishment of the husband and economic background of the wife important, as well as the social role and personalities of each, but the subcultures of their birth and ascent are also decisive in sorting out the successful from the unsuccessful.

Fathers, Sons, and Personalities of the Birth Elite

The birth elite must, during their careers, mark out for themselves substantial business success and discharge social and community obligations they cannot ignore. While the mobile man can be relatively oblivious to his role in the broader non-business community without totally frustrating his mobility, his son and the sons of other business leaders find themselves pressed further by the communities they live in to play central roles in social and civic affairs. This too is a part of their inheritance and part of their task.

The men of the birth elite do not face these responsibilities unequipped. Elaborate education, in private schools and the best universities, is provided along with informal experiences that help fill out their background as proper successors to positions of power. The entire surroundings they come to know, their home, friends, the parties they attend and the sports they take part in, serve to train and equip them for the role of gracefully and effectively wielding social power.

Through all of this, however, the central and overriding fact in the life of the man who is trained and expected to take his father's place is the figure of the father—often energetic, ambitious, successful, dominant, demanding. To succeed easily to the father's position, this man must be able, ambitious, and energetic. He must be on the whole an independent person who can function in a position of major responsibility. At the same time, he must be willing to subordinate himself to his father as an adult and limit his personal drive to the role his family and its social status assign to him.

The conflicts involved in this task are clear enough. By no means all of the sons of business leaders—even those with the necessary qualities for succession—are able to resolve the inherent difficulties of this adjustment. The business elite by its nature does not include the men who are totally unable to make an adjustment to the problem of occupational succession as it confronts men in American business. All of the men studied are business men, functioning with some effectiveness as business leaders. Therefore, in looking at these cases to learn the factors involved in occupational inheritance, it is important to keep in mind that the extreme of this group is not included. Nonetheless, the social and personal issues are clear enough.

Spencer Morgan is president of Morgan Metal Works, Inc., a firm founded by his grandfather in the eighties, that enjoys a continued high reputation. Socially his memberships and activities are appropriate to his and his family's position in the history of the community. When asked by the interviewer about clubs and associations, he said, "Oh, I belong to the Athletic Club, and the Commercial Club, the West Hill Country Club, and Meadowbrook Country Club. And there are some lunch clubs and things like that but they don't mean much. I don't give much time to them. There are a bunch of nice fellows in them, but—." He asked his secretary for a list of organizations to which he belongs and mentioned a few of the names and positions. These included a hospital, the Association of Commerce, the board of directors of a bank, and the Citizens' Commission on Education.

Morgan's wife is also active in community affairs, as president of the Art Club, and board member of St. Andrew's Hospital. He told the interviewer he is sure she is in other organizations, but that he can't recall the names. Mrs. Morgan's father was an investment banker who later became a member of the Federal Reserve Board. Together, the couple represent economic and social power and prestige at a high level.

It was difficult to contact Mr. Morgan, and repeated telephoning resulted in repeated delays in meeting him to discuss the study and his career. The interviewer remarks about their conversation, "In some ways I was more uneasy with him than usual. Throughout the interview there was an undertone of 'hurrying-up' and of nervousness. He constantly turned a small carved paper-weight about in his hands as we talked."

The interviewer asked about the company and Morgan's role in it, and he said, "The family doesn't own the company any more; it's now part of U.S. Steel. I would say almost all of it. There's still a little out, and I think that will be turned up within a year." He gave some background on the company. "My grandfather founded the company back in the eighties. He was president and chairman of the board over forty years." On the grandfather's death, Spencer Morgan's father took over and the company continued to prosper under him. On the death of the father, shortly before the war, Morgan assumed the presidency, with a break during the war while he was in service. "We haven't any stock in it now. We sold, not having any children in the business, and we wanted to diversify our interests. A family company can't exist today. We had to face the facts."

Whatever the facts of the sale of the firm, Morgan continues as president of what is now a minor subsidiary to a giant firm. He is a business leader still but, rather than continue and augment the family position, he will end the sequence of occupational succession; for, while he may continue in his present role, it is unlikely that his sons will.

Some of this break in the pattern occurred early in Morgan's career. He attended Andover preparatory school. "It was my father's idea that I ought to go there; my father had gone to Andover, too. But there is one thing I ought to say about myself. And that's a kind of lack of confidence I had, and I think I felt it in school too. When I went to school I was interested in athletics but I never got good grades. I read a lot but I doubted my ability." In any event, Morgan did not finish Andover, but dropped out because of illness. He attended another prep school for a year, and finally spent a year at Antioch. "I went there because I could use all of my credits. I really never had much education. I left college after two terms; I never regretted it. I learned a lot in business and took some courses afterward. If I hadn't gone into business then I wouldn't have been able to take over the company when I did."

At first Morgan got a job in another metal fabrication firm, but a year later at his father's urging he joined the family firm. "Basically I was a salesman, but I did everything. I worked in the office, and in the mill during the summer when sales were slow. I got a sampling of almost every job. It was my father's idea that I should get all of this experience."

The army seems to have been the high point of Morgan's life. "Having always worked in a family company, the army gave me a chance to compete. I never knew if my position in the company was due to my efforts or my connections. In military life I was sure." This army background came up early in the interview and was the last thing discussed in the interview. "I got my commission without having relations or a drag in the army. If you're interested in the business careers you ought to find out more about the army careers. I worked for three years harder than I've ever worked." Morgan was a colonel on leaving service and listed for the interviewer an imposing series of decorations from several governments as a result of his work in the quartermaster corps.

The impingement of the father on Morgan's life (except in the army) showed up in terms of the school he attended—and did not complete—and the job he took—and has now sold out. The father's presence persists in other areas. "They [his parents] were opposed to my marriage. They objected strenuously. My father said it wouldn't last." In terms of the company, "There is a basic difference between father and son in many businesses. It was the same here. I felt that either I was being pushed too much or not enough." Morgan described more of himself than he perhaps intended as he continued, "I believe there are few businesses where it is carried from the father to the son. In the children of successful business men you often find that the drive and ambition necessary to carry the business on is lacking—not always but often. If they would have to get out and work, like their successful fathers, then it would be different; not all of them would be successful but at least they would be ambitious. I believe that often children who follow their father in successful businesses are resentful because they are afraid they can't make the grade. There are some who take the course of least resistance and others who don't want to live in the shadow of the old man." Asked where he placed himself, Morgan replied, "Frankly, I don't know if I would have accomplished as much, but it would have been a damn sight easier. We were looked on as interlopers in the plant; there was a lot of resentment." To this must be added the fact that the firm has been sold.

Spencer Morgan seems to be living occupationally and socially on the capital invested by his grandfather and father. His son is a student of English and is teaching in a preparatory school in the East. The continuity is tenuous and will not outlast the present generation.

The solution that this member of the birth elite has chosen to the problem of social stability is essentially self-defeating. As one type of resolution among the several available to the sons of business leaders, the case points up the primary problem these successful men face: they must remain within a given social position, they must restate and reinforce the position of their fathers, and at the same time they must themselves be successful and effective individuals.

Among the sons of successful men, this study can only obliquely examine possible solutions to the problem beyond that of entering the father's business. Many of the brothers of the men of the birth elite are in the professions. These occupations, medicine and law especially, make it possible, without loss of social position, to pursue a successful career. Some go into other businesses. But the great majority are in the family firm. The convergence of expectation, training, and pressure makes it nearly impossible for these men to reject the family pattern.

An example of one kind of negative solution is given by one of these men as he describes his brother. "He's not regularly employed. He worked for an investment firm. Now he's in Europe, writing. No, he hasn't been published. I don't know—he's not frightfully well-adjusted. Nothing particularly wrong, but I suspect he's not very happy. I really don't know why he's different. Maybe it is something about not being brought up correctly; maybe he was born that way. Possibly it was too strict a bringing-up—not too strict, but being pushed when little. There's not much meeting ground between my father and brother. I shouldn't imply that there's anything black-sheepy about him; he's not a drunkard or anything like that. I have no objection to his not going into business. There's just no point to his life. He's supported by my father."

The demands on these men that cause them to go into the family business are constant and considerable. That the alternative course of a career in the professions has its difficulties is shown by another of the business leaders in describing his career:

"I never had any compelling ambitions. I went into law because

I wasn't satisfied with what I was doing in the company. I was restless. I was in a good solid firm on the Street for nine years; in fact it's the same firm our U.S. Senator was in—he was there at the time. Then after the war was over I went into the family business. I was older and maybe wiser. I'm more adjusted to life now than I was as a lawyer, but whether it's due to a change in job or maturity, I don't know. I know I reacted more tensely to trial work in law. There was a clear-cut sense of defeat if you got licked, and I worried more about a few hundred dollars that might be involved in a case than I do about thousands in the family business.

"But given the same set of circumstances I would probably do it again that way. Still, some of the advantages of this have been less than the satisfactions of a profession. My advice to a young person today is to find a job that would permit him to express himself—something that would really absorb him. Some lawyers have it, some doctors, too."

This business leader has reluctantly taken his place in the family firm. His legal training serves him and the firm well, but he has not found in business activities the kind of independent satisfactions he would like. He is not an empire-builder but is concerned with continuing the business affairs of the family as he found them.

Leaving aside the question of the careers and goals of those sons of business leaders who do not move into the family business, we see at least two kinds of adjustment to the problem of inheritance of position. There is first of all the business man, now in the position his father occupied, who, like Spencer Morgan, is a prisoner of his past, his family, and especially his father. We find this man in danger of failing, as he is unable or unwilling to accommodate to the demands his position places on him. In the case of the one-time lawyer, now the family firm's vice president, a series of tacit compromises appears to have been worked out. The son takes it upon himself to perpetuate the statuses he has inherited but does not continue the expansion of status or of power.

The problem of assuming successfully the status of the father is most difficult for the son of the mobile man. In a brief candid admission, one of these men simply said, "I'll never be quite the guy my father was." For the men whose occupational succession is a family matter of meeting the expectations of the family in a business that has been built over several generations, the figure of the father does not loom so ominously large. The study of the mobile men, however, indicated the great demands which they place on their sons. A study confined to present-day business leaders does not include those sons of mobile men who found the task of succession difficult. In the cases where the sons of mobile men have succeeded to the father's business position, some knowledge is gained of the difficulties encountered. The comments of one of these men follow:

"I guess I was torn between the desire to start something on my own, to make a name for myself, and the fact that I like what I'm doing and it's more secure. My father worked his way through the University of Kansas and he got the highest grades ever gotten there. And he's proud of it yet. He set the pace for me. He persuaded me to go there, even though I got a scholarship to another university. He's a very persuasive and strict guy; there was a lot of pressure. It's not a good thing. I recommended to my brother not to get caught in it the way I did."

One of the reasons the sons of mobile men find their positions difficult concerns the nature of the father's success. Since the father was first and last a business man, he was not able to establish for himself and his family a high status role in the community that would parallel his business position. The son, to meet the demands of succession, has three tasks: he must first of all yield to the father to the extent that he will undergo the kind of training and early job experience that succession to the father's position requires. In this, he must be able and willing to subordinate himself to his father, to take a lesser and dependent role in the family and in the business.

However, to fill the business role his father has held, the son of the mobile man who continues and augments his father's position must become a self-sufficient business leader, able ultimately to take over from the father and independently and competently direct the business affairs. Further, he must be able to participate in the community in such a way as to establish the family as a powerful and important one. In the case of the man whose college problems were just cited, the process has involved a continual drive, with energy and purpose to match his ambitious and successful father's.

"My father was a strong personality. He tried to influence everybody to his way of thinking, and succeeded pretty well too. I suppose I admire his singleness of purpose most, his logic and his fortitude, and his tremendous guts in the face of any kind of situation. But he didn't know how to relax. He had to support his mother and brothers until they could support themselves, and so he was always very serious minded. By and large I believe both of my parents are pretty well satisfied with me. I suppose I got my business drive from my father and my interest in people from my mother. My father and I don't always see eye to eye on a lot of things, but I go ahead and do them anyway. But I've always had to prove to myself that I was as good as he. That's why the outside activities. I had better than an even break in business but not outside it. I'm still trying to prove myself in civic activities. Actually in the past twenty or thirty years the business has shifted from an odd-jobbing business which was virtually a nonentity to a manufacturing business that's as big as anything in its field. I'm as responsible for the change as anyone, but I doubt if my father or anyone else would admit it. But in the civic world I can prove myself. I can do *that* without a leaning post."

These several examples of sons of business leaders who fail to maintain and re-establish a top-level business and social position, or who experience substantial difficulties in this process, point up the basic dilemmas and some types of outcomes. In some of the cases of men in the birth elite, the resolutions of these problems lead to an integration of personal and public roles, as business leader and community leader of the highest order. A study of the career and personal life of Gordon Curtis provides an illustration of how this process operates.

In terms of his early career, the work history of Gordon Curtis is not unlike that of many of the mobile men. "I didn't have many jobs before I was through school. I worked some on the farm we had as a summer home in northern New York. I believe I have done everything on a farm from plowing to harvesting. Then I went to Yale with some idea of being a doctor. But I decided to quit pre-med after about three years and went into the radio business. I was in the business of selling, service, and managing an outlet for about three years. I quit because I ran into one of the financial services that showed that two thirds of the outlets were going bankrupt in a year. I thought I might be a success with my own agency, but the company might fail. So I went with the company."

Curtis did not move into a top position in the family firm immediately, and his description of this career with the company might well have been given by a member of the mobile elite. The elements of rapid movement from place to place, of constant drive toward his personal goals, and of continued training and learning, are all in his career description. "I spent about a year in Kansas City, in the yards, learning the basic processes, all the different departments, learning how the various products are made. Then I went to Montana for about six months and did the same thing there. Three months I spent at our largest plant, in Wisconsin, still training. Then I went to the Chicago office as a junior clerk. I became manager of the department in 1933. Here's where there was a certain amount of luck. The former manager failed. He got into financial difficulty, and failed as a manager. I was then made conscious of the importance of *knowing* the person in the job; his personal integrity and knowledge are very important. Then in 1938, one of the vice presidents died suddenly and I became vice president. There were three or four people better equipped for the job that I got. They didn't have the will to get up and go. One of them particularly could have gone ahead with his ability. But he lacked nerve. You could actually see his knees shake when the boss yelled at him."

The firm was founded by Gordon Curtis' great-grandfather and a partner who was soon bought out. The family continues to own the largest single block of stock, but holdings in the company are widely distributed. "My father took it for granted that I would go into the business eventually." For all of this, Curtis continued to drive hard in his work. During the war he played a part in the functioning of OPA as a department head. "I had a lot of experience in Washington in various production lines. After I returned I moved into more general administrative duties, and in 1951 I was made president of the company."

Curtis' drive is by no means exhausted. "A business has to expand; it can't stand still. I can't think of anything I'd rather do than what I am doing. If I were to do it over again, I'd probably make the same errors, and I would hope I'd make the same successes. Of course my main plan is just to try to see that the company prospers and continues to grow, that it holds the respect it has today and improves on that. As to the future, if we can develop the right type of young men, who might take hold when the top offices open up in a few years, it would be better for the company. I don't want the day-to-day, minute-to-minute direction of the thing. There's nothing more important than getting the team to work together under a good coach."

The general contours of this career outline are similar to those of the mobile men, in terms of drive, goal-orientation, energy, and ability and readiness to move geographically. However, some differences are clear. Curtis tends to see his future more in terms of the company and its success. There is no question as to his self-confidence and assurance; still he looks to the future in a less personal, more long-range fashion than the mobile men are able to do.

With this concentrated business activity has gone a good deal of community activity. Curtis is a member of many organizations, social, philanthropic, and business. He is a university trustee. He is involved with fund-raising for cancer research. He functions as a member of the State Republican Finance Committee. He is a board member of a trade association. "Occasionally I take part in the Boy Scouts, and I used to do Community Fund work regularly. I'm a member of the board of Junior Achievement. I am very interested in this movement which helps young high school students get started in business. Through it they learn something about running a business. I guess those are the more important ones; that is, the ones I am most interested in."

The business success and high social position represented by Mr. and Mrs. Curtis appear against a background of social stability and continuity. They now live in a fashionable suburb of Cleveland, where Mr. Curtis was born. He described, with no exaggeration, his family circumstances as "very comfortable. We had one or two maids, plus a cook and a nurse." His mother's father was a merchant who came to Cleveland when it was still a village. Grandparents figured large in the family activities Curtis remembers from his youth. The oldest of four children, Curtis attended a New England preparatory school and then Yale, as had his father. Curtis and his wife had known each other for fifteen years, from summer vacations where the two families had homes in the same area. Asked how his parents felt about the marriage he said, "They were very, very happy; they're very close. Our mothers were friends; they still are, and visit each other often."

This member of the birth elite presents a kind of integrated and stable life history not found in the examples of the business elite presented thus far. Geographically and socially he has been, on the whole, stable. His marriage and family are interwoven into all of his activities in a way that is impossible for the mobile man by definition. The past and the future function for Curtis as a meaningful part of the present. He is an energetic and probably tough business man, yet aware of his inheritance and his responsibilities to the future. Far from leaving the past or denying it, he is concerned with building on it. Consistent with this he says of his sons, "I hope that one will come into the business at least. They've got to develop as they go through college—trusting that they get in. The oldest one had to write a theme for school on what he will do when he gets older and he said he would go to work for the company. It depends entirely on the circumstances when they're ready."

Like most members of the birth elite, Curtis was easily accessible to the interviewer, pleasant and relaxed. Typically, he did not choose to be interviewed at home, maintaining the privacy his social status has given him. This unobtrusive privacy extended in the case of Curtis at least to his discussion of the persons in his life. Somewhat like the mobile men interviewed, he was chary with details of his relations to his parents especially.

Of his father, Curtis said, "My father was much more serious and earnest in his approach to life than mother. My father was a combination of idealism and matter-of-fact practical approach. Mother was more spiritual, more emotional. My father was a direct person, impatient with obstacles. He had tremendous energy, although he was a rather frail-appearing man. He was courageous in any stand he took; a very intelligent sort of person. I have a terrific admiration for him; his capacities were tremendous. In my mind he was a great man, much beyond whatever I could hope to be. I always had a sort of defeatist attitude. I'm glad I had the advantage he gave me, and have wanted to take advantage of it, but I have always been determined to do it my way."

These remarks about the father nicely combine what appear to be the two necessary but not easily compatible elements in attitude toward father on the part of these men who succeed to the father's position. Curtis is first of all apparently thoughtful and, presumably, realistic in his assessment of his father as direct and energetic. He cites his respect for the father. But, most important, he finally strongly states his independence, and re-affirms it in his responses to the Thematic Apperception Test. The analysis of the TAT summarizes his feelings about his father as follows:

Curtis' relations with his father are marked by reserve and caution. At no point does he give any indication of close or warm relations with, or feelings toward, his father. Rather he portrays the father as a basically helpful figure, not at all punishing, but as someone who is approached on a rather impersonal basis. He is willing to listen to the father and recognizes the abilities of the father, but very strongly emphasizes his own need to reach conclusions and take action as a separate person. The manner of reaching these conclusions is curious, and is repeated, probably representing a deep-seated pattern in the father-son relationship. The son is shown as impetuous and emotional. The father is a controlling and advising figure, but the advice serves as a brake on the son's behavior, and is not accepted immediately. Only on reflection, and after action, is the father seen to be right.

Considering the interpersonal attitudes of Curtis in contrast to those of the mobile men, essential similarities and differences appear in the TAT. Like the successfully mobile man, Curtis portrays himself as independent and self-directing. He poses problems on his own terms and wants to seek out his own solutions. Thus, he portrays most relationships—with father, mother, and friends—as subject to change, and sees that it is necessary to leave, to become an independent person.

At the same time, in working out his independence and in making his break with people, Curtis and the men of the birth elite like him strive to make these changes and achieve independence in a manner that does not permanently break off all contact with the people. He is sensitive, as the mobile men are not, to the consequences of his behavior for others and tries to find solutions to problems that will meet his own needs while respecting the basic ties and feelings people have about each other.

To be mobile, the men who move through long social distances must be able to separate themselves readily and easily from other people. They must direct themselves with total concentration to their personal goals, with little attention and less concern for other objects or persons. The task and psychological equipment of the men who successfully inherit their social position and build on it are different. Something of the same capacity for separation from other persons must be present, but the solutions must be worked out in terms of continuing relations with the past and the people in the past.

Parents and Children: Earned and Unearned Privilege and Power

We cannot show by statistical measurement how the effect of birth into the elite aids or hinders the son's career in business, nor the degree to which it contributes to success. However, we do have evidence on the relation of the accumulated power and prestige of the family to business achievement.

The occupational and family backgrounds of the business leader, as we have seen, are important in shaping his career. The kind of education he receives or achieves, the kind of woman he marries, the kind of jobs he takes—on his career road, the way he moves through the country—all are affected directly or indirectly by the occupation of his father, which is one indicator of the kind of family he comes from. Just how occupational and family backgrounds affect the many phases of the life career are more difficult to determine than the simple fact of correlation. But in one area, the career of the son in the same firm as the father, the elements of the story are nearer the surface.

Family factors influence occupational succession in ways other than actually bringing the son into the same firm with the expectation that he will succeed to his father's position. How are such influences expressed? Do certain social institutions such as families and friends, rather than economic ones, increase the likelihood of some occupational groups' advancing themselves more than would be expected if such factors as skill, ability, and the like were the only ones involved?

What kinds of men do and do not receive help? Are men with relatives in the firm advantaged or disadvantaged? Do such men climb to the top more rapidly than others or are there no differences? Do those with connections reach higher positions more often than those less well placed? How does 1952 compare with

1928 in regard to the social and family influences that impede or expedite the development of a business career?

The degree to which a family affects the career varies with the family's status. Many of the business leaders who have been mobile from the bottom, or near the bottom, have rejected their families and climbed up and away from them. They have rejected that way of life which, far from helping them, would impede their progress or make it impossible. Men born to the elite, on the other hand, have families who, for the most part, expect them to go to college, expect them to stay in high position, reinforce their careers with social and economic power. Because of the interlacing of family power through many industries, one often hears the rather cynical comment that it is not *what* you know but *whom* you know that counts in getting ahead. Less cynical and perhaps a little more realistic is the comment that a friend can only get you in the door—from then on you're on your own. Those born to the elite who have had to compete for their jobs find that "shirtsleeves to shirtsleeves in three generations" can be all too true; that no business can afford to hire and advance men who cannot compete with the most ruthless and strongest competitors.

Just what the family influences are on the life career of the business leader is difficult to probe quantitatively for the whole group of men studied; however, we have a number of measurements which, correlated with such known factors as influential relatives, friends, or financial aid, give us considerable insight.

The number of years required to reach business leadership is one objective measurement. Influential friends in the firm seem to make little difference in the time it takes the leader to achieve top position. But when relatives are present, the average years for achievement are 19 or 20 compared with 23.8 for the whole group.

What were the backgrounds of the leaders so benefited by influential relatives? The percentage of those having no influential connections in the same firm is closely correlated with the status of the family, those of low family status having the largest percentage with no friends or relatives in the firm. Between

8 and 9 out of every 10 sons of skilled or unskilled laborers or farmers were without such help and between 7 and 8 sons of clerks or small business owners, compared with only 3 or 4 sons of major executives or owners of large businesses. Turning this around and looking at those who did have relatives in the same firm we find that all occupational backgrounds are slightly represented except owners of large business and major executives; over a third to almost one half of their sons were so benefited.

Executive positions in large industrial empires are more powerful posts than the top positions in smaller industries. What does this measure of prestige add to our knowledge of the influence of relatives in a business leader's success? Clearly, as the size of the firm increases, fewer leaders have influential friends or relatives in the firm. About a third of the leaders who are in smaller firms, under $10 million, have friends or relatives present, compared with less than a tenth of those in large firms, over $250 million.

For our whole group of business leaders, in each category of position and size of firm, the difference in age at reaching the top was small, and this was not affected by the presence of influential friends or relatives in the firm. One can only conclude that the multiple factors entering a man's life through the years average out timewise.

It will be recalled that 52 per cent of all the elite studied were the sons of business men. Forty-three per cent of these are in a firm where their fathers were either owners or major executives. This is almost as much as in 1928 when 45 per cent of this birth elite were in the same firms as their fathers. But this broad comparison obscures certain significant differences which are revealed when we distinguish between major executives and large owners, in the occupational background: In 1928, 49 per cent of the sons of major executives were in the same firm, compared to 40 per cent today; but 41 per cent of the sons of owners were in the same firm, compared to 60 per cent today. More sons of executives go elsewhere to make their careers, but even more sons of owners stay in the family firm where they enjoy the greatest advantage.

Type and size of business affect recruitment and advancement policies. Smaller enterprises seem to foster the "inheritance" of the father's position, whether he is owner or top executive; the larger enterprises are less favorable to inherited position. As the size of the firm decreases there is a steady increase in the percentage of owners' and managers' sons in the same firm: from one fourth to two thirds for the former and from one tenth to seven tenths, almost three fourths, for the latter. In the smallest three grades, half or more of the sons of major executives are in the same firm as the father.

When we compare these figures with a generation ago, we find that in every size type of business except the smallest, the proportions of sons of major executives or owners actually decreased up to 1952. The increase referred to above for sons of owners is accounted for by the enormous increase in the smallest type of enterprise, and this alone; all others decreased.

Type of industry also enters into the picture. The proportion of sons in the father's business ranges from one fifth in the retail and wholesale trade to none in public utilities communication. Those having the highest proportions are real estate, wood and coal products, personal services, and security and commodity brokers; those with the least, public utilities communication, oil, gas and coal products, railroads and other transportation, banking and finance, electrical machinery, chemicals, stone, clay and allied products. The factors operating here are the strong traditions within an industry regarding who the management will be—some feeling that positions should be filled by the most capable regardless of kinship, some opposing nepotism, some wanting the son to learn the father's business and keep it within the family.

To be factual in all details, of course, one cannot state the relationship of sons to types or size of firms in such categorical terms. Some businesses have grown up too recently to see what generation pattern they will follow. Also, large firms in general give more opportunity to the young man with ability and no influential connections; but because they are so large and their management hierarchy so ramified, there are many opportunities for fathers and sons to be in the same organization.

Compared with a generation ago, there are fewer sons holding the top positions of president or owner in the same firms as their fathers. But this figure, which has fallen by one half, is more than offset by the increase in sons among vice presidents and below. This is undoubtedly due to the changing organization of business itself, the increased size and complexity of each enterprise demanding someone to head up each phase of operation with the title of vice president and reporting to the overall management.

None of these considerations changes the fact that the stronghold of inherited position in America today is the smaller, family-dominated enterprise. However, the center of power lies in the large corporations where men of ability are encouraged and rewarded to rise to positions of top management and where influence of family or friends can gain a member of the birth elite entrance to the race, but it won't help him run and it won't help him win.

When we were discussing the influence of relatives in the same firm on the career of the business leader, the measurement used to test advantage was the number of years required to reach present position. We found that the average achievement time was 19 or 20 years for those with relatives in the same firm and 23.8 for those without. If a business leader is in a firm in which his father occupies, or has occupied, a high position, what is the effect on his career? Does he fill an important office on his first arrival on the job or must he, too, devote a substantial period of his life to attaining high status? How long does it take?

Using the same measurement, achievement time, to answer these questions, we examined the records of all of the sons of minor and major executives and small and large owners and found that the average acheivement time for all of the sons in this group who were in the same firm was accelerated from 2.5 to 6 years over that of the sons not in the same firm. The sons of owners, large or small, had a much greater advantage than the sons of managers—6 years compared to 2.5. The achievement time ranged from 15.7 years, for sons of large owners who were in the same firm as their fathers, to 22.1 years for the sons of minor executives in the same firm. These figures for that portion of the birth elite who are especially favored by being in the same firm as their fathers compare with the mean of 24.7 years for the achievement time of the mobile business leaders.

The distribution of our 1952 business leaders through many occupational backgrounds would indicate that not many of them had the advantage of sizable inheritance or even of gifts and loans, despite the general attitude that the men who are at the top of our business world must have had help that others were denied. Only 6 per cent of the total group received financial aid of any kind. The influence of this group, however, should not be depreciated because of its size, for it is an important and significant segment of American life. Who are they?

The proportion of sons of major executives and large owners who received financial aid (17 per cent) was almost three times the percentage for the whole group of business leaders; it was three times the number of professionals' sons and over five times that of sons of small business men and farmers, with white-collar sons and sons of laborers trailing. "To him who hath shall be given" is borne out by the fact that the men who were benefited by being in the same firm as their fathers were also most benefited by financial aid: 28 per cent of this group received such help. This is another measure of the contrast between the roads traveled by the birth elite and those who are mobile.

Who were the people from whom these men received financial assistance, and how was it done? Only a small percentage received help from friends; the balance was almost evenly divided between relatives and inheritance.

A generation ago twice as many of the business leaders received financial aid as today; the drop has occurred in all occupational groups and types of assistance, but is larger among the sons of major executives and large business owners, both in inheritances and in help from friends or relatives. In order not to confine ourselves to occupational background alone, we studied financial aid in relation to size of business enterprise and found that, though the diminution since the last generation has occurred in all sizes of enterprises, the loss has been sustained in the largest enterprises, A, B, and C, and that sons of "small" owners in the categories of enterprises D and E, below the $50-million mark, have actually gained. But this does not affect the only possible deduction from these figures, that money, while still a powerful aid to many, is of decreasing significance in the kind of competition that exists in our business world today.

9

Men in Motion:
The Circulation of the Leaders

In the rich and powerful array of symbols expressing what America has been and would become, those representing geographic movement and physical space are no less potent and meaningful than the symbols which reinforce our belief in opportunity and equality. The *Mayflower* and Ellis Island, the Conestoga wagon and the clipper ships, the Model-T and the motel—these and many others evoke the migration, movement, and change that color and characterize the American experience. The list is long— "Pike's Peak or bust," the 49'ers and the Oklahoma land rush, greenhorns, tenderfeet, and sod-busters—each speaking of men and groups of men constantly arriving, leaving, and again arriving. Note the trailer camp, and ask what other nation would take for granted so large a proportion of its own people living, well and happily, constantly on wheels. No other nation of the West has used space as a dimension of its life in like manner.

This readiness, even need, to move spatially, rooted deep in the history and behavior of Americans, is a major part of the total mobility pattern of the American people, interwoven with their continuing and endless changes in social position. Indeed, in the legends of business success and social mobility that express the American Dream, movement through physical space of the men memorialized is an integral part of the total pattern of their lives and careers. "America is the land of opportunity"; and the figure of the immigrant struggling against odds of education, manner,

177

and birth, through to success—the Andrew Carnegie story—expresses the Dream for the immigrant and for his son.

Small-town and farm backgrounds are an important element in many of these legendary careers, of which the Wendell Willkie story is a recent example. The farm boy storming the big city conveys a special sense of moral propriety, as the basic virtues formed by the simple rural life triumph over sophistication in the success legends. When a big-city editor trumpeted "Go West, young man," he expressed a common belief that by moving in geographic space, social movement would follow in the course of affairs.

The business leaders, like the nation whose commerce they direct, are men on the move. Changes in location and residence are a dimension of their lives no less meaningful than the changes in social position they have experienced, and this spatial mobility plays an important part in determining the nature and patterns of occupational mobility in American business. To a large extent, these leaders are determined by geographic factors, working with factors of social background.

The place in which a man is born geographically, as well as socially, helps to determine the social position he will come to occupy in his career. Not all parts of the nation—regions and states—produce business leaders in equal proportion. Men born in big cities have different mobility chances from men born in small towns. The Yankee and the Southerner, the small-town boy and the city boy, the native-born and the foreign-born—who play a special role in the mobility process—all share differently in "equality of opportunity" in American business.

Where the Men of the Elite Come from

All parts of the United States, and foreign nations as well, supply members to the business elite. Ninety-five per cent of the present-day American business leaders were born in the United States, and, while all sections of the country are represented in the group, almost two thirds were born in the fourteen states making up the area east of the Mississippi and north of the Ohio rivers. Over a fourth of the men of the business elite were born in New York, Pennsylvania, and New Jersey—the Middle Atlantic region; and almost as many in Ohio, Indiana, Illinois, Michigan, and Wisconsin—the East North Central region. This group of states, the

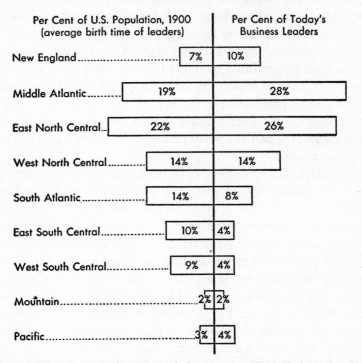

Per Cent of U.S. Population, 1900 (average birth time of leaders)	Per Cent of Today's Business Leaders
New England............................... 7%	10%
Middle Atlantic.......... 19%	28%
East North Central... 22%	26%
West North Central............ 14%	14%
South Atlantic.................... 14%	8%
East South Central.................... 10%	4%
West South Central.................... 9%	4%
Mountain....................................... 2%	2%
Pacific.. 3%	4%

Chart VIII.   From What Part of the Country Did Today's Leaders Come?

highly industrialized sector extending from the Eastern seaboard through the Great Lakes area, is the recruitment source for over half of the total business elite. New England accounts for an additional 10 per cent; the Southern states, including Oklahoma and Texas, only 16; and the West North Central region, including the Dakotas, Minnesota, Iowa, Missouri, Nebraska, and Kansas, about

14. The Mountain states and the Far Western states produce only a small portion (see Chart VIII).

In order for these figures to tell an accurate story, we have to know how they compare with the general population of these areas. The continuing migrations of the past fifty years within the country have changed the population picture to the extent that the 1900 census, the average birth time of our present leaders, gives the best comparative figures.

In the Middle Atlantic and East North Central states, the areas which together produced more than half of our present elite, the figures for business leaders exceeded the proportion of these areas in the general population; in the West North Central states there was a balance; the Pacific Coast showed a higher proportion for business leaders; and the Mountain states are in balance, but the figures are small.

In general, the productivity of the regions in business leaders parallels the economic and industrial development of the regions. Until recent years the Southern states have lagged considerably behind the general industrial level of the nation. This limitation, combined with a generally lower standard of education, no doubt plays its part in this result. Another possible factor in the South, more speculative, may be a tendency for young men of higher-status backgrounds and advanced formal education to enter other than business careers. For example, recruitment by the armed forces has generally been high in the South; tradition, military schools, and economic conditions may well combine to lead potential Southern leadership into military careers. Politics may offer a similar opportunity, in contrast to other sectors of the country. But changes in the industrial development of the South, coupled with a breakdown of the area's traditional isolation from the rest of the country, might well lead to an increase in Southern representation in the business elite in the future.

The poor showing of the South may be due in part to the presence of Negroes, a group which swells the population figures but has so far been prevented from adding to the proportion of leaders. The same argument, however, could be used to contend that the labors of this group would serve to liberate the energies of the top group for leadership activities. In following up these arguments we found that the under-representation of Southern-born men extends through all occupational groups in about the same proportions, which puts the question back in the general social context we have already suggested.

Regions that Lose Their Leaders

The birthplace for most of the men of the business elite is only a point of departure for the series of moves that pattern their careers. In this movement, certain regions lose some of the leadership they produced, and others, of course, gain. Ten per cent of the leaders were born in New England, for example, but only 7 per cent remain; whereas on the Pacific Coast, where only 4 per cent of the leaders were born, there are twice as many today. These gains and losses in business leadership reflect corresponding gains and losses in the commerical and industrial growth of these areas.

The Middle Atlantic states show an increase from 28 per cent of leaders born there to 38 per cent living there today. The Southern and Mountain regions show some decline, but less to be expected, the Great Plains states show the largest single decline—from 14 per cent born there to 9 per cent there today.

The regions of the nation may be broadly grouped into those that gain in leadership potential at the expense of other regions, and those that are the supply areas for these regions. The first group includes the Middle Atlantic states (see Chart IX). They show an increase of 73 per cent over the number of leaders born there, of whom three fourths have remained. Washington, Oregon, and California, the Pacific states, also are high in retaining leaders born there.

The East North Central states tend to retain their business leaders and show only a slight diminution in net numbers. The remaining regions retain less than half of the men born there.

This movement of men out of some areas into others in the

course of their careers occurs in systematic ways. For example, over half of the leaders born in New England moved out into the Middle Atlantic states and down the Eastern seaboard but not

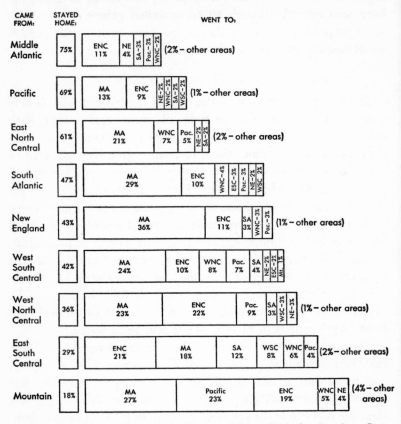

Chart IX.   After They Left Home, Where Did the Leaders Go?

into other sections of the country. The limited movement into New England is primarily from the Middle Atlantic states.

The West North Central states also lose much of their potential leadership. It tends to move west, to the Mountain states and the Pacific Coast, with a limited amount to the adjacent

Southern and Eastern states. This is a westward-looking area in terms of mobility career patterns (see Chart IX).

Movement out of the Mountain states is in large proportion westward also, to the Pacific Coast, although this area also supplies leadership in fair proportion to the Midwest and East. There is a reciprocal interaction between the Mountain and Pacific states similar to that between New England and the Middle Atlantic states.

Patterns of movement between and out of the Southern regions are more general. The East South Central region looks primarily to the Southwest and its leaders tend to move in that direction, probably into the petroleum industry. There is considerable interchange among the Southern regions, but also a fair distribution of Southern-born throughout the entire nation.

While there are patterns to the movement between regions, basically all regions are available to men born everywhere. Differences between regions exist primarily in terms of their rates of production of business leaders and the degree to which each region retains its potential leaders.

The Geography of Occupational Mobility

These two kinds of movement of the American people— spatial movement, from place to place, and social movement, from one social position to another—are significant elements in the mobility patterns of the men who make up our business elite. The two types of movement are interrelated in varying ways. We will consider them against the background of the combined factors of region of birth and occupation of father.

If we take the five primary occupational backgrounds—of business men, professional men, white-collar workers, laborers, and farmers—and four broad areas, North, Midwest, South, and West, as regions of birth, we have twenty types of background. Among these the rate of social mobility is highest for sons of Midwestern business men and lowest for sons of Southern laborers: the sons of Midwestern business men are members of the business elite in nearly 7 times their proportions in the population, while the representation of sons of Southern farmers is less than one fifth the expected proportion. The sons of Northern business men are almost as likely to enter the business elite as sons of Midwestern business men, and sons of Midwestern and Northern professional men follow, with 4 times their proportion of the population.

Sons of business men are highly represented in the business elite, but in the South and West their ratio is less than 4 compared with a ratio of nearly 6 for the country as a whole. These figures, like all others, of course, express not simply a matter of less opportunity but also a tendency in these areas for men of this occupational background to go into other than business activities. Sons of professional men in these areas have a low ratio also—it may well be that in the expanding West especially many men remain in the professions of their fathers.

Only two other groups are represented in the business elite in larger—though only slightly larger—proportions than in the total population: the sons of Midwestern and Northern white-collar workers. This regional ratio compares with a little over 1 for the country as a whole and indicates, probably, that the urban factor is involved and that access to educational facilities and business activity stimulates the mobility rate of white-collar sons in this area.

All remaining occupational-geographic groups are under-represented in the business elite. Southern and Western laboring backgrounds, along with Southern and Western farm backgrounds, are least likely to produce business leaders, with a rate of about one fifth of their representation in the general population.

The fact that sons of farmers are less likely than men from other backgrounds to move to business leadership has already been remarked on. However, when farm background is considered along with regional background, it develops that the sons of farmers from the North especially, and also from the Midwest, are more likely to become business leaders than the sons of laborers from these areas. That is, farm background is not in its nature a nearly insurmountable barrier to mobility into the business elite; rather, it tends to bring with it a series of factors—cultural milieu, standard of living and education, and others—that may also be associated with other backgrounds in even greater degree.

Small Towns, Big Cities, and Business Leaders

The small town and rural countryside represent in the minds of most Americans the more lasting and simple virtues of a less

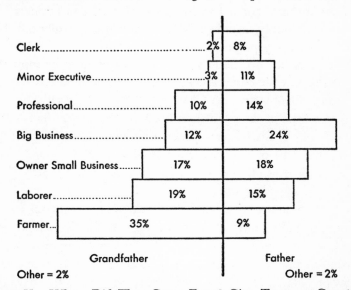

	Grandfather	Father
Clerk	2%	8%
Minor Executive	3%	11%
Professional	10%	14%
Big Business	12%	24%
Owner Small Business	17%	18%
Laborer	19%	15%
Farmer	35%	9%

Other = 2%   Other = 2%

Chart X. Where Did They Come From? City, Town, or Country?

complex and anxious past. The youth of the small towns are held to represent in higher degree the morality and abilities that will be rewarded by success.

To this somewhat wistful evaluation of the small town the social psychologist has added a rationale for the conclusion that the product of the smaller communities is more likely to be successfully mobile. The cities tend to congregate their classes in separate areas, where people with different ways of life, whether resulting from nativity, income, race, or religion, are relatively isolated from one another. It has been maintained that the children born into these areas do not have the models in their communities from whom to learn the kinds of behaviors necessary to a mobile career. They lack, it is argued, the patterns on which to mold their own style of life different from that of their own families. In this view, the more heterogeneous small city or town, including in a single limited area persons of all types, incomes, and life-styles, increases the probability of mobility. The small-town boy, in more intimate contact with the professional and business men of the community, may in this view learn more readily the skills and techniques appropriate to a higher status.

The argument is persuasive, but does not seem to be supported by the facts of the business elite. The typical business leader is not born in a small town (see Chart X) but in a large city. In 1900, only one third of the population lived in the metropolitan centers but a fourth of the business leaders were born there. On the other hand, over half of the population lived in rural areas and towns with populations of 2500 or less in 1900, but only a fourth of the business leaders were born there.

For the country as a whole, the relationship between size of birthplace and representation in the business elite is a simple one: the larger the community, the greater the probability of membership in the business elite; but there is variation by region. For cities of 100,000 population or more, there is little difference between the regions. The large cities of each region produce business leaders in about the same proportions. For cities of 25,000 to 100,000 population, however, regional differences are somewhat greater. Cities of this size in the Midwest, more than in other regions, are most likely to produce future business leaders, and those in the North least likely. This may well be related to industrial expansion, for in the past half century cities of this size in the Midwest have increased notably in industrialization. In the Northern states, however, the recent example of the migration of the textile industry out of moderate-sized New England cities serves as a reminder of changes in the industrial strength of many of these communities.

The smaller communities, those with populations under 25,000, and rural areas, show one important regional difference. As noted, these smaller communities in general produce a smaller proportion of business leaders than would be expected from their total population. There is little difference between North, Midwest, and West in this respect, but in the South these communities are under-represented to a marked degree.

These elements in the geographic background of the business elite indicate that the typical member of the business elite in the United States is born in the North or Midwest. He is a big-city man, born and trained in the large population centers, the son of a business or professional man. While no single group seen in terms of these factors is excluded from the business elite, there are some rare types. Most rare is the Southern small-town or country boy, son of a laborer or farmer, for the man from the Southern farm is by all odds least likely to enter the business elite—he does not have access to higher level positions in American business and industry today.

The Men Who Move

It is not a coincidence that in this nation, where social position is more fluid than in other societies, physical mobility is more characteristic of the way of life than in any other urban society. The total and almost immediate acceptance of the automobile as basic and necessary reflects the deeply rooted demands for mobility which produced the restless migrations in our history. Geographic space is a dimension of our social life as functional as rank and status.

In some ways the discussion of geography and the business elite thus far has been misleading. It is important to an understanding of the nature of the business system and its leaders to recognize that birth in many areas of the country substantially reduces mobility chances; but it is also true that all regions and communities are part of the system of movement that leads to business leadership.

The varieties of geographic movement among the men of the business elite defy listing, but some of the more obvious are already clear. Business leaders who come in part from the small towns and countryside move to the larger cities sometimes in their own states, sometimes in another state, and sometimes in another region of the country. Some men, in the course of their careers— when attending school or while beginning their job histories, for example—leave the state in which they were born but subsequently return to the city or state of birth. Movement from one large city to another within the boundaries of a single state is also common.

Four groups can be separated and contrasted on the basis of geographic movement. Well over half of the present-day business elite are now located in a state other than that in which they were born. An additional 7 per cent are from rural backgrounds (population less than 2500) whose rural to urban mobility took place within the state of birth. Together these groups make up more than two thirds of the total business leadership. Forty-five per cent now are located in a *region* different from that in which they were born.

The figure of approximately one third of the business leaders who are geographically stable in the sense of now residing in the state in which they were born is in contrast with the figure of 77 per cent for the U.S. native-born population who were residing in their state of birth in 1940. It would appear that the business leaders are about twice as mobile geographically as the American population. In the light of the fairly high migration rate in the population, this amount of geographic mobility is very high indeed.

The amount and extent of geographic movement are related to the size of birthplace. Over half of the elite born in large cities are living in the state in which they were born; almost three quarters of those from rural backgrounds have moved out of their state of birth.

In examining the possible relation between ocupational background and geographic mobility we find the sons of farmers more often territorially mobile, as would be expected. The least mobile groups are first of all sons of big business men, and, next, sons of laborers. The explanation for this last lies in the fact that within a large city a relatively short geographic move may place enormous social distance between the individual and his background.

The son of a laborer who becomes a business leader must leave his place of birth socially and territorially as part of the total movement process. He can move enormous distances without leaving the metropolitan center in which he was born. He can place between himself and his point of birth the necessary and inevitable geographic distance by moving only a limited number of miles. The son of a laborer born on Chicago's South Halsted Street who moves to Lake Forest has moved farther in every sense except number of miles than the man born in Lake Forest who moves to Westchester County.

Thus, the men of the business elite are mobile not only in the social distance they have traveled from their social birth position, but also in the geographic distance they have traveled. The two great currents of movement in America—through social and through physical space—are intertwined into a single process. Each depends upon the other; each derives much of its existence from the other. It has been argued that this combination of geographic and social mobility was a unique product of the Western frontier of an earlier America. But the role of the frontier in maintaining our society as a flexible and open one was simply one symptom of an underlying and basic fact of our social system. The frontier did not cause social mobility, nor did mobility decrease with the passing of the physical frontier. The movement westward of the American people was one expression of an enormous, continuing restlessness that propels them from one place to another across the face of the nation. This movement, encouraged by geography and augmented by technology, is a precondition of social mobility. The web of relations, holding individuals in their birth positions in social and physical space, is constantly broken, and reordered, by the capacity and desire of the individual American to change all aspects of his social position, of which geographic location is but a part.

The Immigrant and Business Leadership

The impact of geographic movement on social mobility in America can be seen directly in the most dramatic kind of mobility, the immigration into America of large numbers of foreign-born workers. About 5 per cent of the American business elite are foreign-born; about 20 per cent are U.S.-born sons of foreign-born fathers; the remaining 75 per cent are at least third-generation Americans.

What do these proportions reveal of the "melting-pot" theory? The forms of disadvantage and discrimination suffered by the foreign-born in adjusting to American society are legion, and it is not to be expected that positions in the business elite would be easily accessible to the immigrant, nor even to his son. That the disadvantage of the foreign-born in achieving top business positions is considerable may be inferred from the fact that, while nearly 10 per cent of the U.S. population are foreign-born, less than half that proportion, or about 5 per cent, of the business elite, are foreign-born.

This disadvantage does not persist over the generations, for the sons of foreign-born men make up the same proportion (one fifth) of the U.S. white population (in 1940) and of the business elite. In a single generation the disadvantage of foreign birth in achieving top business positions disappears. Sons of foreign-born men are as likely to enter the business elite as sons of native-born. The "melting pot" operates rapidly and effectively, it seems. Personal motivation and family training combine with the educational system and the informal training on the job to shape the sons of foreign-born men quickly into the pattern of behaviors and skills that project them to the top levels of American business.

Not only does the disadvantage of immigrant background quickly disappear, but there actually are more mobile men among the "new Americans" than among the "old Americans." The stable men, the sons of business and professional men, make up the bulk of the "old American" group. Forty-two per cent of those men whose fathers and fathers' fathers were born in America are the sons of big business or professional men, and only 10 per cent are sons of laborers. In contrast, 24 per cent of the foreign-born

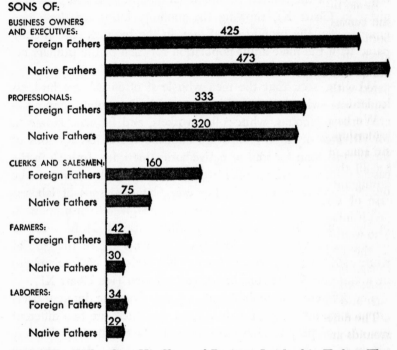

SONS OF:

BUSINESS OWNERS
AND EXECUTIVES:
Foreign Fathers   425

Native Fathers   473

PROFESSIONALS:
Foreign Fathers   333

Native Fathers   320

CLERKS AND SALESMEN:
Foreign Fathers   160

Native Fathers   75

FARMERS:
Foreign Fathers   42

Native Fathers   30

LABORERS:
Foreign Fathers   34

Native Fathers   29

Chart XI.   Who Gets His Share of Business Leadership Today? The Sons of Immigrants or the Sons of the Native Born? (Figures Represent Mobility Ratio.)

fathers were laborers, and only 26 per cent were big business or professional men.

In other words, there actually is more mobility among the second generation men than among the men whose families have been in America for several generations. Far from conferring a disadvantage, immigrant backgrounds serve a positive advantage in the mobility process. Somehow, these sons of immigrants move to top-level positions in business in larger proportion than do the sons of old Americans from lower-status backgrounds.

Some measure of this tendency can be obtained by comparing the census data for sons of foreign-born men with sons of U.S.-born men in the primary occupational groups. This comparison is given in Chart XI, showing the mobility ratios for these two groups when the proportion of men in the business elite is compared with the male adult population for each of the primary occupational groupings.

We have seen that the men who least often achieve business leadership—who are most disadvantaged in the mobility process—are sons of laborers, white-collar workers, and farmers. However, for all three of these groups the disadvantage is less for sons of immigrants than for sons of native-born Americans. Indeed, in the case of sons of white-collar workers—clerks and salesmen—the disadvantage does not exist. For every hundred sons of laborers who would be expected in the business elite, given their proportion in the population, the actual mobility ratio is 34 for sons of foreign-born men and 29 for sons of native-born. In the case of white-collar workers, the ratios are 160 for sons of foreign-born men and only 75 for sons of native-born men (see Chart XI).

The differences in mobility rate for men from the different backgrounds are not so great as to suggest that these are two different universes of people. However, given the fact that there is every reason to assume that immigrant background would operate to a disadvantage for the son of a laborer, clerical worker, or farmer, even equal mobility rates for sons of foreign- and native-born men would be rather surprising. In fact, the advantage in mobility ratio is with the immigrant's son.

From this unexpected and apparently puzzling fact, it is possible to retrace the mobility process to establish a better understanding of what social mobility consists of and the meaning of geographic movement in the process. For mobility to occur, it is necessary that the many emotional and social engagements and obligations holding an individual to his social position and place be broken off.

Consider the man born in a small community, the home of his family for generations. The house he lives in, the streets he walks, the parish he belongs to, his neighbors, his occupation—in short, the entire pattern of his life—most intimately intertwines the past with the present and future. Except for a war-born catastrophe, his relations in space and through time form a pattern of commitments, engagements, and obligations binding him to the physical and social space to which he is born.

Such a man might live in India, in Western Europe, in the Kentucky hills, or in New England. A whole spectrum of such communities, each less time-bound than the next, might be arranged; they would have the common quality of stability, and of a pattern of life in which even small changes in life-style, in associations, in economic activities, and in social relations would be conspicuously remarked, and remarkable. This web of relations is the product of extensive social usage and of generations of time. Movement out of such a system, even the most extreme, is possible, but the difficulties of such movement are compounded geometrically as the web of relations is elaborated.

The meaning and role of the elaborate spatial movement in the careers of business leaders now become more clear. If we put aside all questions of ambition, talent, and opportunity, and look simply at the movement itself—its nature and the difficulties it presents— we see the place of spatial movement in the mobility process. The son of the immigrant is that man least engaged with the past. He is to an extreme degree disengaged. To become part of American society he must turn his manner from that of his father, who in turn had undergone the experience of shattering the web of relations holding men to their social positions as he migrated to America. Wherever they might go, whatever their social destination, the sons of immigrants are *par excellence* men on the move, whether they will it or not. The preconditions for movement upward in the social system are established for these men. To a degree, this same condition of potential social mobility exists for all persons in American society. To the extent that this is a restless nation, where men move from place to place easily, and children learn to accept such movement as a part of their normal life experience, the conditions are established upon which the factors of emotional need, ambition and motivation, talents and techniques which make up the mobility process may operate.

Thus, the two great sources of the changing face of the nation are part of the same system of change and fluidity. The restless migrations and propensity for physical movement of the American people are a necessary precondition to the changes in social position that make up the reality underlying the American Dream.

It is probable that the rapid, drastic, and continuous movement through the space and the institutions of their society would leave distinguishing marks on the world view of the men of the business elite. Men who leave their natal communities, their families of origin, and their social past are in many ways set free. The movement they undergo will leave them free upon their arrival in the elite from the kinds of obligations to people and institutions that characterize men whose roots go deep in their communities. They are free to a singular degree to act in an impersonal and rational manner in their new environments, learning their sets of traditions and moves and adapting to them quickly as part of the mobility process.

The unique rationalization and impersonalization of action and outlook that seem to differentiate the men in American business management from those of other nations no doubt are due in large part, to this freedom from unquestioned custom. These men by their geographic mobility are in many ways made independent of the past; entering new situations—new communities, new companies, new people—they can adopt sets of attitudes toward them unencumbered by the traditions of their early training and previous environment.

Separation from the past in social and physical space enables mobile men to act as innovators and to accept and put in motion new ideas and methods in their business activities. Much of the unique strength of American business management is due in part to geographic mobility, the separation from the web of relations, as these men move.

To these probable results of geographic movement other out-comes must be added. The separation from social past and social origins which contributes to rational and impersonal behavior in business management (sometimes good, sometimes not) may well foster an illusion of self-containment—a sense of self-sufficiency and isolation—that works to the disadvantage of the community.

The rapid movement of these men through space may give them a view of their careers as self-controlled and self-contained. When the total career has been worked out in the close relations and recognized obligations of a single community, responsibilities must be recognized. When the individual moves rapidly from one situation to another—when, for example, he leaves the community that reared him before realizing the kinds of social and personal debts the rearing has incurred—he is not likely to feel that sense of community indebtedness that could make him a responsible and serious community leader.

Men for whom the past is a point of departure, serving only as a measure of the distance traveled, will be prone to view themselves as the products of their own ambitions and training. It is not fashionable to speak today of self-made men, yet the underlying meaning of the phrase and its significance in terms of how the speaker sees himself remain real. No social being is self-made, and even the imputation is an absurdity; the successful mobile business leader is a product of his society as surely as his mediocre counter-parts, the failures, and all the rest. The implications for the effects of this self-perception on behavior are unpleasant. Self-made men owe no debts—to their fellows, their community, or their sub-ordinates. Self-made men are not likely to seek to preserve the values of the past when working to create the future. It is in such experiences as geographic mobility and separation from the past that this illusion of self-containment is fostered. Restlessness lead-ing to movement may also foster rootlessness, social and emotional. The consequences in the behavior and attitudes of some of the men who occupy elite positions may well be indifference to the values and beliefs of the past, and to the needs and debts they owe their communities.

10

The Business World
and the Business Career

Although the common experiences, training, and viewpoint of American business men make it possible to consider them as a single group, and the business world as a fairly homogeneous unit, business leaders differ from each other in important respects— types of companies and industries in which they have worked out their careers, for example, and other aspects of the career pattern.

Differences in the kinds of companies these men direct are an important element in shaping the social pattern of the business elite. American business and industry is not a single unit, but a loosely bound and far-flung system of activities. Each type of business and industry includes companies that differ from each other in important respects. The differences examined include:

1. Frontier types of business and industry: How does the growth of a company, and of the industry in which it operates, affect the kinds of business leaders in these companies? Is there a frontier in business, made up of new and fast-growing industries? Does the ambitious man have a better chance with a fast-growing company? Or should he join a new company to improve his opportunities?

2. Open and closed industries: To what extent is leadership in certain types of business and industry closed to all but college graduates, or sons of business leaders? Which types of business and industry offer the best chance for the mobile man and for the self-trained man? Where does the man from the South and West move to the top?

3. The elite within the business elite: Is there more opportunity

in the smaller companies? Granted that sons of laborers, farmers, and white-collar workers go high in the business world, how far can they go? Are the positions of chairman of the board and president open to them, and in which kinds of companies?

In addition to differences within the business world with respect to mobility and opportunity, important differences exist among business leaders as to the kinds of careers they have experienced, the pattern of jobs they have held as they move to business leadership, and the length of time they have spent in their careers before achieving top positions. These questions about the business world and the business career can be answered at least in part through the study of the business elite.

Frontiers in Business and Industry

Ours is a nation in which constant growth, movement, and expansion have come to be a necessary part of the image we must have of what our country is. The closing of the frontier and the exhaustion of the lands of promise to the West in which new lives and new ideas could flourish brought much uneasiness. If the dream of ever-increasing and always equal opportunity is to be kept meaningful, something like the Western frontier must exist. A new area is always needed where one may escape from the realities of one's social world, the realities which contradict the dream. The new areas—frontiers or eras, space or time— promise the revitalization of the dream.

As the Western frontier closed, images of new frontiers were envisioned in the new business firms and new types of business and industry which science and enterprise have combined to produce in considerable numbers in the twentieth century. These business frontiers are held to offer the opportunity once believed to exist in the new lands, and to offer to ambitious young men the same kinds of opportunities.

To learn the extent to which expanding firms and industries offer increased opportunity for mobility, the 1952 business elite was studied in terms of two kinds of business growth: (1) rapidly expanding *types* of business and industry were compared with moderately expanding *types* and those that have remained stable or shown a loss relative to their size in 1929; (2) rapidly growing *companies* were compared with moderately growing *companies* and those that have experienced little if any growth over the past two decades. The background and training of the business leaders in these types of business and industry and in the type of individual companies were compared.

The kinds of business and industry included in these categories of slow, moderate, and rapid expansion reflect the concept of the business frontier fairly well. In the rapidly expanding group are the petroleum and chemical industries, trucking and aircraft, radio and television, for example. In the moderately expanding group are furniture, rubber, and apparel manufacturing, insurance, and construction. The relatively stable group includes mining, banking, railroads, textiles, utilities, and others whose size relative to the total economy has remained fairly stable over the past two decades.

Within each of these types of industry and business are individual firms that may have shown slow, moderate, or rapid gains. These two factors, type of business and type of company, must be considered together in examining the concept of the frontier. If there is a business frontier in this sense, and if this frontier accelerates the mobility process, then the greatest proportion of sons of laborers and white-collar workers would be expected in the rapidly growing firms in rapidly growing industries. At the same time the greatest proportion of sons of business and professional men would be expected in the slowly expanding firms in relatively stable industries.

The facts show that a business frontier seems to be a reality only in a limited sense. The two factors of expansion of company and expansion of industry do not work together to effect the rise of men from lower-status backgrounds to business leadership. However, when type of company alone is considered we find that more sons of laborers and farmers and proportionately fewer sons of major executives and large business owners are leaders of rapidly expanding firms. More sons of executives and large owners are leaders of the more stable companies. The differences are not sufficient, however, to justify the argument that growth of company greatly affects occupational mobility.

The differences are even less when expansion of type of business or industry is examined. For example, 13 per cent of the leaders of slowly expanding firms in slowly expanding types of business are sons of laborers. The same proportion of sons of laborers are leaders of slowly expanding firms in rapidly growing industries. In terms of mobility chances, the notion of a frontier in business seems to be a myth.

However, the growth of the company or industry does have a marked effect on the process by which the individual becomes a leader in the industry. It will be recalled that about 13 per cent of the business leaders did not graduate from high school, about 30 per cent had some college, and about 57 per cent are college graduates. In the fast-growing companies in new and expanding industries, 22 per cent of the business leaders did not finish high school and only 44 per cent are college graduates. In the most stable firms—slow-growing companies in stable types of industry— only 6 per cent of the leaders failed to finish high school and two thirds are college graduates. This rather close relationship between kind of education and growth of company is true for all types of business expansion (see Table IV).

Mobility for the man with little formal education into leadership in a stable, slow-growing business is rare. This kind of business is staffed, for the most part, with men who have completed a college education and acquired a maximum of formal training. It may well be that the old, stable, well-established firms, secure in their competitive positions within the industry, more frequently use formal procedures in selecting potential leaders. These are the firms that look to the Ivy League "for the right kind of man" and tend to value social graces, manners, and other qualifications not directly or obviously connected with the job. Moreover, these firms

TABLE IV.   THE RELATION OF EDUCATION TO BUSINESS EXPANSION
(*in percentages*)

Expansion of Industry	Expansion of Firm	Less than High School Graduate	High School Graduate or Some College	College Graduate	Total
	Slow	6	27	67	100
Slow	Moderate	10	27	63	100
	Rapid	14	32	54	100
	Slow	9	32	59	100
Moderate	Moderate	13	32	55	100
	Rapid	23	38	39	100
	Slow	10	24	66	100
Rapid	Moderate	13	31	56	100
	Rapid	22	34	44	100
All businesses		13	30	57	100

more frequently have established a pattern of training and career movement through which aspiring executives move.

The more rapidly expanding companies and industries more frequently are led by men with little formal education. These companies may well place greater emphasis on occupational skills related to the job—experience with a technical process, a background of supervision and job training, and familiarity with the company and industry. There is also the probability that rapidly expanding industries have not developed the formal requirements for potential leaders nor the formal mechanisms of leadership movement. In their need to obtain and promote men promptly, they emphasize the kinds of skills and training acquired outside the formal educational institutions, with less attention to background and social manners.

The self-made man, or the man who would become self-made, does indeed find a frontier in rapidly expanding businesses. This frontier is not related to the background from which he comes but to the kind of training experiences he has had.

Another item in this area to be considered is the age of the firm. When business leaders of firms established since 1928-1929 are compared with men in the older firms, few differences of background or career are evident. Age of firm alone has little relationship with the mobility process.

Open and Closed Industries

The leaders included in our study were drawn from the total range of American business and industry. Expansion of the company or industry is only one of the complexities of this universe. The single term, business and industry, covers the whole range from coal and oil industries through banking and retail stores to hotels and management consultant firms. Our business leaders show disparities as great as those between the investment banker and the trucking tycoon. In terms of the mobility and training of the leaders, we wondered if some businesses were a sort of private preserve, in which only a certain kind of man from a certain kind of background is allowed to move up to leadership, while others are an open hunting ground, where every man is free to move on his own merits, skills, and qualities.

Out of the welter of differences, some ordered grouping of businesses can be arranged on the basis of kinds of activities. For purposes of this study, twenty-six groupings were established, each fairly distinct from the other, while still covering a sufficiently broad range of activities to make the grouping significant. A kind of scorecard of mobility can be established ranking the business groups from those relatively closed to men from lower-status backgrounds to those in which a good deal of mobility from the factory, office, and farm takes place.

This scoreboard is given in Table V. For ease of examination, sons of major executives, professional men, and owners of large businesses are combined into one kind of occupational background. The businesses are listed in order, from the smallest to those with the largest percentage of sons of big business and professional men.

It is not surprising to find that investment banking, and the general category of brokers and dealers, is in a class by itself, with

TABLE V. IN WHAT INDUSTRIES IS THERE THE MOST AND LEAST MOBILITY?
(in percentages)

Business Group	All Occupations except Major Executive and Owners	Major Executive, Owner Large Business, Professional	Owner Small Business	White Collar	Laborer	Farmer	Total
All groups of business	62	38	18	20	15	9	100
I. The most mobility:							
Electrical machinery	74	26	19	23	22	10	100
Oil and gas	72	28	24	20	14	14	100
II. Second highest mobility:							
Insurance	64	36	15	27	10	12	100
Food and tobacco manufacturing	65	35	18	21	14	12	100
Transportation equipment manufacturing	67	33	18	22	17	10	100
Public utilities and communication	69	31	19	23	16	11	100
Mining	69	31	18	24	13	14	100
Railroads	70	30	11	22	23	14	100
Highway transportation	70	30	12	23	25	10	100
III. Average mobility:							
Miscellaneous manufacturing	61	39	22	17	17	5	100
Chemicals and allied products	61	39	22	18	11	10	100

TABLE V, CONTINUED

Business Group	All Occupations except Major Executive and Owners	Major Executive, Owner Large Business, Professional	Owner Small Business	White Collar	Laborer	Farmer	Total
Construction and engineering	61	39	20	18	14	9	100
Personal services	62	38	17	20	20	5	100
Machinery manufacturing	63	37	22	20	12	9	100
Wood products and furniture	63	37	20	19	18	6	100
IV. *Below average mobility:*							
Paper and allied products	57	43	21	19	13	4	100
Real estate	58	42	22	16	10	10	100
Metals and their products	58	42	15	19	17	7	100
Glass, stone, and clay products	58	42	16	19	17	6	100
Trade, wholesale and retail	59	41	19	16	15	9	100
Miscellaneous transportation	59	41	10	29	12	8	100
Business services	59	41	21	18	15	5	100
Textiles and apparel	60	40	21	18	15	6	100
Printing and publishing	60	40	17	22	16	5	100
Banking and miscellaneous	60	40	18	19	14	9	100
V. *Least mobility:*							
Brokers and dealers	42	58	14	18	8	2	100

over half, 58 per cent, of its leaders the sons of big business and professional men (Group V). This compares with an average percentage of 38 for leaders of this background in all businesses. More than any other business, the brokers and dealers category may be considered relatively closed to men from lower-status occupational backgrounds.

At the other extreme, several categories of businesses have relatively few sons of big business and professional men in positions of leadership. Men from these backgrounds make up less than a third of the total leadership in several industries including utilities and communications, mining, railroads, highway transportation, the petroleum industry, and electrical machinery manufacturing. This illustrates well the fact that mobility and opportunity are not related in any simple way to expansion or age of industry. One might expect utilities, especially railroads—old, well-established, relatively non-competitive industries—to be least accessible to mobile men. In fact, the proportion of men whose fathers were big business or professional men is lower in railroads than in most other businesses.

Sons of small business owners, who made up 18 per cent of the total business elite, appear in fairly regular proportions in all businesses, confirming the view that this is an intermediate and pivotal group, in the whole mobility process, from which movement in almost any direction will take place. However, few sons of small business men appear in railroad management. This same rather even distribution obtains for sons of white-collar workers, with the amendment that a rather high proportion appears in executive positions with insurance firms.

Sons of laborers make up a larger proportion (one fourth) of the total leadership of railroad and highway transportation companies than of any other kind of business. Only 8 per cent of the leaders of brokerage and investment houses are sons of laborers. The odds on the sons of farmers becoming leading brokers and dealers are slight indeed, for they make up only 2 per cent of the leadership in that group. They comprise 14 per cent of the total leadership of mining, railroads, and the petroleum industry.

Education is also related to kind of business in the extent to which the business or industry is "open" or "closed" in mobility terms and the extent to which it is a "technical" one, requiring detailed and formal technological skills.

Brokers and dealers again appear as a "closed" category: 71 per cent of the executives are college graduates and only 8 per cent are less than high school graduates. However, the chemical and paper manufacturing industries are even more dominated by advanced education, with 77 and 72 per cent of their leaders college graduates. The proportion of business leaders who did not graduate from high school exceeds 20 per cent in only two industries, railroads and highway transportation, which appear to be the most "open," where the man from a low-status background and with little formal education is most likely to achieve business leadership.

A further aspect of the influence of kind of business on mobility has to do with the region in which the business leaders were born. The broker and dealer group is dominated (60 per cent) by men born in the North—New England, New York, Pennsylvania, and New Jersey. Over half of the leaders in food and wood products manufacturing are from the Midwest; generally the Midwestern states rank high as region of birth of leaders in most of the manufacturing industries.

The South, with its generally low level of representation among the business elite, supplies its largest proportions of leadership to mining, railroads, wood products, petroleum, and textiles—industries to which Southern men would have most ready access. The Western states contribute their largest proportion of leadership to real estate and construction—consistent with the recent growth and expansion of the region—to the petroleum and trucking industries, and, less understandably, to the broker and dealer group.

Occupational background, education, and region of birth seem to have a rather consistent effect upon the leadership of certain kinds of business and industry. Brokers and dealers least represent the ideal of an "open" economy. Leaders in this category of business are most likely to be sons of big business or professional men, born in the Northern states, and college graduates, and least likely to be sons of laborers, with little formal education, born in the Midwest or South.

Railroads and highway transportation stand in sharpest contrast to this relatively closed sector of the economy. Here the men who are least likely of all to become business leaders appear in largest proportion—men with relatively little formal education, sons of laborers and farmers, born in the South and West. Although they have this point in common, these two industries are in sharp contrast in many ways—the railroads stable, conservative, well-entrenched, and the bus lines and trucking concerns, new, dynamic, and rapidly changing.

Public utilities and communications are intermediate between these extremes. Many men from non-business, non-professional backgrounds are leaders in this field, but for the most part they are college trained, and tend to be from the Northeastern states. In construction and engineering, leaders are drawn rather typically from all occupational backgrounds, tend to have a college education, and tend to come in fair proportion from the South and West. Leaders in real estate include relatively few sons of white-collar workers or laborers and fewer college graduates; region of birth seems to have little relationship with business leadership in this category.

From this scorecard of mobility expectancy by kind of business, we can see that the overall rate of mobility into the American business elite is in part a composite of many factors that are at work in the business arena in which these mobile careers are carried out. Technological level of the industry, geographic distribution of the industry, doubtless the differing financial and social histories of the several kinds of business, organizational differences, rate of growth and expansion—all of these and many other factors interplay in establishing the rate of social mobility which measures the extent to which an industry is "open" or "closed."

The Elite within the Business Elite

The type of position the business leader occupies in his firm is also a distinguishing feature of his career. The men included in the study are all members of the top level of American business. This level is a single unit when looked at in the context of the broader groupings of rank and position within business as a whole, but, when examined alone, the business elite includes men of many different ranks. Many of the bases for ranking these men—intangible factors relating to influence, power, and prestige—could not be measured by the methods of this research. Two factors that affect the rank of the men within the business elite are available for study, however: the size of the business in which the leader holds his position and the position he occupies in his firm. These factors play an important part in determining rank within the elite and make it possible to examine the question of the extent to which there may be said to exist an elite within the elite.

The past three decades in particular have seen the giant corporations move to dominance of the business scene in a manner certainly not envisioned in the trust-busting era preceding World War I. Much has been written to lament or applaud the workings of these corporations on the national scene. How do the giant corporations affect this mobility process? Are they inherently non-egalitarian, tending to increase occupational rigidity, as they do price and production rigidity? The American Dream of equal opportunity has as a minor theme a concept of the independent entrepreneur, the enterprising small business man who builds for himself a large firm. This man is well-nigh absent, in reality, from American business on any considerable scale. Has his absence depressed the overall mobility rate? Will continued business consolidation work to reduce occupational mobility?

Size of company can be considered along with business position to establish a rank order within the total elite group, from the higher positions in larger firms to the lesser ones in relatively smaller firms. The question is whether mobility to, say, chairman of the board of a firm with annual sales of a billion dollars is less accessible to the mobile man—a more closed position—than, for example, vice president or treasurer of a firm with $10 million annual sales.

As with growth of business, the analysis of mobility of the business elite on the basis of achieved position is not simple. A higher proportion of sons of laborers appears in the positions of secretary, treasurer, and controller than in the vice-president group. Similarly, more vice presidents are sons of laborers than are chief executives—presidents, chairmen of the board, and owners and partners. This same relationship is true for the sons of white-collar workers and farmers. The higher business positions are occupied in proportionately larger numbers by sons of big business men. Sons of professional men and owners of small businesses appear in about the same proportions in all levels of business position.

To a degree, the more highly ranked business positions are more difficult of access, less frequently achieved by men from lower-status backgrounds. Mobility takes place to all levels of business positions but less often to the topmost positions than to those at a lower level.

However, when business size is considered a somewhat different relationship is found to exist. The proportion of sons of major business executives and owners of large business is substantially smaller in the larger business firms than in the smaller business firms studied. There is more occupational mobility in the largest business firms than in firms of smaller size.

Fourteen per cent of the business elite in firms with less than $10 million annual gross volume are sons of laborers, and 30 per cent are sons of big business men. In the larger firms, those with a gross volume of more than $250 million per year, 16 per cent are sons of laborers, and only 19 per cent sons of big business men. Sons of owners of small businesses appear in about the same proportions in all sizes of firms. However, sons of white-collar workers increase from 15 per cent in the smaller category to 21 in the larger, and sons of farmers also show a corresponding increase with size of business.

There is an elite group within the business elite. Sons of big business men occupy more than one third of all chief-executive positions studied. However, it is not true that there is less opportunity or mobility in the biggest business firms. On the contrary, the larger firms more often are led by men from lower-status backgrounds.

This result would appear to augur well for continued openness in the American business system. The rise of the great corporate structures, accompanied as it has been by a decline in individual ownership, has apparently increased rather than decreased the mobility potential. This suggests that the image of maximum mobility in a business system where competitive conditions are maximized is oversimplified. The process of mobility is not a simple function of competition. The rationalization of business and industry and the increased depersonalization of the organizational structure resulting from the rise of giant corporations serve to minimize the influence of family associations on leadership selection and, under existing conditions, increase recruitment from all status levels.

To compare the present day with a generation ago: in both periods there was less occupational mobility into higher positions than into lower positions; more sons of business men assumed top positions. Differences between the two time periods are not great. However, a higher proportion of sons of laborers occupy the second-level business positions at the present time than in the former period, while the proportion of sons of big business and professional men in positions of chief executive has increased somewhat. It would seem that the top positions have become more difficult of access, though the difference is slight. A greater accessibility of second-level positions to sons of lower-status men may well account for a good deal of the slight increase in occupational mobility observed between 1928 and 1952. Those positions, including vice presidents, financial and legal officials of the companies, are filled in larger proportion by these mobile men.

A study of education and business position illuminates the meaning of this trend to some extent. There has been in the business elite a trend to higher formal education at all levels. It may well be that, as a result of the increased availability of formal education (and its social concomitants in manners, style of life, and friends and associations), men from lower-status backgrounds are able to acquire a high level of formal and technical skills that aid them in competing for second-level positions where these skills are most highly valued.

Age, Time, and the Business Career

Along with the differences within the business elite in the business setting, the patterns of the careers differ both with respect to age-time dimensions and in the types of occupations moved through on the way to business eminence.

The typical member of the present-day business elite is almost 54 years old. He entered business just before his twenty-second birthday and became associated with his present firm 7 years later. He has been with this firm for 24 years. He achieved his present position 24 years after entering business and has held it for almost 7 years. The typical business career begins between 21 and 22, with a period of shifting between jobs and companies until at about 29 years of age the future business leader joins the firm he will eventually come to direct. He is 45 or 46 years old before he achieves his position of leadership.

These average figures mask great diversity in the group. The men of the business elite range in age from their early thirties to over 80. Many have spent their entire careers with a single company, in some cases a period of over 45 years. A few, well-favored and influential, move almost directly into top positions and have occupied them for over 25 years. In other cases it is 40 years or more before real eminence is achieved in business.

These great differences in age factors and in career timing are a result, of course, of differences in background, circumstance, and training; the differences among the several groups in the business elite in terms of career timing provide a measure of the career advantages and disadvantages of background and training. The youngest group in the business elite are the sons of major executives, with an average age of slightly over 50; the oldest are sons of farmers, with an average of 56 years. These differences in present age between the backgrounds reflect differences both in the age at which the business career is begun and in the length of time required to achieve a leadership position.

The sons of laborers enter business at the earliest average age, between 18 and 19 years; sons of major executives do not enter business until they are over 21, on the average. Sons of laborers require 26 years to achieve present position, sons of farmers and white-collar workers, 25, and sons of major executives, less than 21. Men from higher-status backgrounds enter business later and achieve top positions in less time thereafter than men of lower status.

The advantages of background combine with those of education and training to reveal marked differences in the timing of the business career. Table VI presents the average age of the leaders when they entered business, the time required to achieve present

TABLE VI. DOES HIGHER EDUCATION REDUCE THE TIME
IT TAKES TO ARRIVE?

Education	Age Entering Business	Time to Achieve Present Position	Present Age
Less than high school	15.3	31.0	60.5
Some high school	17.0	30.6	58.0
High school graduate	18.7	27.9	56.5
Some college	20.3	24.5	52.9
College graduate	22.3	22.9	52.8
College, postgraduate	23.4	19.9	49.8
All business men	21.4	23.9	53.4

position, and average present age, for each of the six education groupings on which information was available.

Men with less than high school education entered the business world when slightly over 15 years old. In sharpest contrast, the men who did postgraduate work at universities did not enter business until more than 23 years of age. Conversely, the men with least formal education required 31 years to achieve their present positions, while the men with the maximum formal education achieved their positions within 20 years of entering business. Finally, the men with less than high school education are more than 60 years old on the average, while the men who engaged in postgraduate study are slightly under 50.

These differences are the culmination of a number of factors. In any group in the population, the older men will have had less education than the younger men. Furthermore, education not only is a measure of kind and length of training but is, of course, closely associated with other advantages of birth and family position which come together with education to cause these age and time differences among the educational groupings.

However, when the age of entering business and years required to achieve present position are combined, the resulting figure— average age of achievement—does not vary greatly; it takes about as long, looking at the life-span, to achieve a top business position for one group as for another.

Equipped with the prerequisites to mobility—motivation, skill, opportunity, and the rest of an undetermined complex—some mobile men achieve their training outside the boundaries of formal education. The process is difficult and few men are motivated, equipped, or impelled to undergo this informal and self-directed training. However, for those who do, the total time for this more difficult process does not greatly exceed that involved in the conventional approach to training and experience. Whether the learning and training take place in office, shop, or college classroom, the span of time required to achieve a top position is singularly similar.

This index may be used to measure the relative impact of other career factors on the timing of the career. For example, the territorial movement involved in many careers lengthens the career time for most men, but the differences are slight indeed, for men who remain in the state in which they were born require an average of 23 years to achieve a top position while those who move to other regions require 24. Territorial movement by itself does not greatly affect the length of the career.

Nativity and length of career are more closely associated. Foreign-born business leaders spent 26 years in achieving their present position, while men whose fathers and grandfathers were born in the United States required only 23 years. As with all other differences, those related to nativity are the result of multiple, interrelated factors—in this case, the country of birth itself, a generally lower-status occupational background, and less formal educational training.

Our present leaders compare with a generation ago in the following ways: The present business elite is a somewhat older group, with an average age of 53.7 years compared with 51.4 years in 1928. There are two reasons for this: fewer young men under 45 (15 per cent of today's leaders), are in present top business positions than earlier (28 per cent in 1928); the proportion of men over 65 has remained the same for both periods, 11 per cent.

The trend has been to compress the age range of the business elite. While fewer young men are included, the older group has not grown larger. The net result is a more limited period of effective leadership available to the business world from these men; the longer training periods lengthen the pre-leadership career, and the conventional retirement age of 65, generally in force, stops the career at the same age as before without regard for the fewer years of active leadership served.

These findings are confirmed by the data on the number of years spent in present positions by the 1952 and 1928 groups of business leaders. Half of the 1928 men had been in their leadership positions for less than ten years, compared with two thirds of the

1952 group. This process is depriving the business hierarchy of a substantial portion of the total leadership potential of these men.

The lengthening of the period spent in training and in business prior to assuming positions of leadership has operated for men from all occupational backgrounds with a general increase in the minimum age of some four to six years, between 1928 and 1952. Only about one year of this total is a result of increased pre-business training, for the 1928 business elite entered business at an average age of 20 years, while the 1952 average is 21 years. The lengthening of the pre-leadership period has taken place largely within the business world proper rather than as a result of a generally increased level of formal education.

Job Patterns in the Business Career

Occupational mobility not only refers to the movement of son as compared with father, but may also refer to the moves from one occupation to another during the lifetime of an individual. These patternings of occupational movements are also related to factors of birth background and training, and their analysis extends the portrait of the business elite.

Apart from the Horatio Alger hero, the popular image of the career of the successful business man seems to include two alternative routes. The first begins with the shop, foundry, or forge—the two-fisted laborer, rough but brilliant, works up the line from the production section through supervision and minor executive posts to top management. Alternatively, and usually in non-manufacturing businesses, the career begins as a salesman, whose tiny capital, invested in a shop of his own, is built by dint of shrewdness, labor, and daring into a mighty empire. Contrasted with these themes, in the popular mind, is the son of the owner who catapults over the entire system into an immediate position of dominance.

These popular stereotypes do exist, of course; the images are not fabricated out of whole cloth. But they form a minor group within the business elite and have been almost entirely superseded—if indeed they ever existed in substantial numbers—by the white-collar career, with movement through the store or office, or one of the professions, by gradual stages and steady progress, into positions of business power. The typical career pattern is a bureaucratic one in business today, just as the typical business organization is primarily bureaucratic. Careers are built largely on formal education, acquisition of management skills in the white-collar hierarchy, and movement through the far-flung systems of technicians and lower-level management personnel into top management. Traces of the legendary patterns remain, and spectacular examples of the type exist; they tend to be unique.

The first occupation of the present-day business elite is shown in Table VII, along with the occupation they held five years before entering business, ten years after, and fifteen years after. Four-

TABLE VII.   How Far Did They Go in Fifteen Years?
(*in percentages*)

Occupation of Business Leader	First Occupation	Five Years Later	Ten Years Later	Fifteen Years Later
Unskilled or semi-skilled laborer	11	1	0	0
Skilled laborer	3	2	1	0
Clerk or retail salesman	34	15	4	1
Salesman	9	10	4	2
Foreman	1	4	3	1
Minor executive	9	35	43	25
Major executive	1	6	26	57
Business owner	1	2	3	3
Engineer	9	8	4	3
Lawyer	6	5	4	3
Other profession	9	8	6	4
Military career	2	2	1	1
Government career	1	1	1	0
Training program in a business firm	3	0	0	0
Other occupation	1	1	0	0
Total	100	100	100	100

teen per cent began their careers as laborers, 43 per cent began as clerks and salesmen, and 24 per cent as professionals. Few at any point in their careers were entrepreneurs in the sense of owning or establishing their own businesses. Also, while there have been a number of cases of men moving from top-level military positions into key business positions of late, these form only a minor proportion of the total business elite.

Not only did few of our leaders begin their careers in the factory but those who did moved rapidly out of these positions. Within five years of beginning, only 7 per cent are either laborers or foremen, and within ten years the proportion drops to 4 per cent. Indeed this rapid movement out of lower-level laboring and white-collar positions is typical of the entire group. Men who are marked for subsequent leadership do not long delay in making their first moves in that direction. The proportion of men occupied as clerks or retail salesmen diminishes by half within the first five-year period to only 15 per cent and drops to 4 per cent within ten years.

Five years after starting the first job, the emphasis is already on management positions, with over a third of the group in minor executive posts. However, the men who begin their careers as professional men—engineers, lawyers, accountants, and so on—do not leave these jobs in substantial proportions until ten years after entering business. This convergence on management positions continues at a fast pace, and within fifteen years of entering business over 80 per cent of these men hold management posts, the majority already major executives.

Characteristically, the careers of the men in the business elite are white-collar and professional careers; moreover, career progress begins soon in their lifetimes, continuing at a steady pace with fairly rapid movement. Presumably the man who early in his career is unable to make a move of some sort occupationally is left behind, unable to recover the ground lost in early delay. The leaders are men who move fast.

These career patterns vary of course by background and education. Sons of laborers do begin their careers in the factory very often (nearly a quarter of the group), and almost half are clerks or retail salesmen. Only 14 per cent begin as professional men.

On the other hand, 25 per cent of the sons of white-collar workers and owners of small businesses begin their careers in the professions. Education and training are more valued, and more readily available, to men from these backgrounds, and the fact is reflected in the emphasis on technical skills implied in this proportion.

Sons of major executives or owners of large businesses are more likely to begin their careers in upper-level white-collar jobs, and a fifth begin their careers as minor executives, but about a tenth begin as laborers. This group does not use the professions as an avenue to business leadership in great proportion. Engineering, for example, is the first occupation of over 10 per cent of the white collar–small business group, but of only 8 per cent of the big business group. The sons of big business men are more apt to go into law than are men from lower-status backgrounds and less likely to enter the other professions.

As would be expected, a large proportion of the sons of professional men begin their business careers in professional occupations—over a third. Sons of professional men enter laboring and sales jobs in about the same proportion as sons of other higher-status groups. The difference lies in the use of the professions rather than jobs as clerks or retail salesmen as an entrance into the business world.

Sons of farmers are also likely to enter business through professional training. The importance of education for mobility from the farm into business is indicated by the high proportion, nearly a third, of sons of farmers who are first engaged in professional occupations. This professional work is most often engineering, accounting, and the like, for only 5 per cent started their careers as lawyers.

Subsequent to the first occupation, the pattern for men from different occupational backgrounds is similar. Consistent with the findings on career age and time, sons of laborers continue in laboring and clerical positions longer than men from other backgrounds. Sons of professional men who enter the professions remain in them for some time. The occupational progression pattern, through the minor executive posts to top management, occurs for men from all backgrounds, and by the tenth year in business 80 per cent of the sons of major executives or owners of large businesses are in the positions of minor or major executive. By this time, also, two thirds of men from all backgrounds are in executive positions.

Education is also related to career pattern, even more closely than occupational origins. Almost a third of the men who did not attend high school were first employed as laborers, and only a tenth of the college graduates; but over a third of the college graduates first held professional positions. The formal company training programs, as expected, are confined almost totally to college graduates.

If in fact, as these career patterns suggest, the public's notion of the careers of top business men is misleading in its emphasis on factory and entrepreneurial backgrounds, the question remains of the extent to which these patterns of business careers have been changing over time. A comparison with 1928 on these points is not possible, but it is possible to compare the younger with the older men in the 1952 group for some indication of time trends.

Comparing the men under 50, 50 to 59, and 60 years of age and over, the proportion of men who begin their careers as laborers is less in the younger groups. The number in white-collar positions is about the same for all three age groups. Fewer of the younger men begin their careers as engineers, and a larger proportion begin as lawyers or in other professional positions. Further, the proportion of men who begin their careers in a training program with a company has more than doubled, from 2 per cent of the older group to 5 per cent of the younger group.

To suggest that these age differences reflect time trends is somewhat misleading, for age is a reflection of background and education, and these differences between the age groups are a function of many factors in addition to the time differences. It does seem likely, however, that the increase in the proportion of men first engaged in formal training programs in business firms does reflect a real change over the past several decades in the patterning of the business career. Training programs appear increasingly to be employed as a primary source of recruitment into top management positions. This development presents some hazards for future mobility rates in business, for the training programs are usually confined to graduates of colleges and universities, in many cases limited and specified.

Thus a company in the past may have drawn its executives from the open market, including hiring them from other companies, selecting men who have worked their way up and shown particular skills in the company itself, and generally emphasizing informal recruitment procedures into executive positions. This company might well today have drawn up a formal training program, admitting only the graduates of certain selected colleges into the program, and using it as the primary source for its executive recruitment. To the extent that these programs are closed off to men from the factory or office, or are limited to the graduates of colleges and universities difficult of access to men from lower-status backgrounds, the effect of these training programs may well be to reduce the amount of occupational mobility into American business in the future.

In terms of social policy, to maximize occupational mobility and to employ in business leadership the skills available through the entire social system, these business training programs need further examination in terms of their future effects on opportunity and mobility in business.

11

The Meanings of the Careers
of the Business Leaders

The Flexible Society and the Free Individual

The careers of contemporary business leaders, when compared with the last generation, tell an important and, in some respects, satisfactory story. Examination of the economic and occupational backgrounds disclosed the number of men who came up from the bottom and the number born to position; it is essentially a stocktaking of fathers and sons to derive an estimate of the present conditions of American life. From this study, meaningful conclusions about the nature and well-being of our society may be drawn; vital precepts emerge to help us judge our conduct, discipline ourselves, and regulate our economic, political, and social life.

The ordered process of occupational succession in Big Business demonstrates that at least in this prestigeful and highly valued part of our economic life our society is somewhat more fluid and flexible than it was yesterday. There is more circulation in and out of the higher and lower statuses; more men from different family backgrounds enter, hold, and leave powerful positions. The fathers of the elite and the ambitious striving men at the bottom both have greater awareness that the principles of birth alone are insufficient for maintaining high status today. Values of achieved status and social mobility are expressed more fully, and those of inherited position less so, than a generation ago.

Admittedly, only a small percentage from the bottom climb to the top, yet this percentage since 1928 has almost doubled. Hereditary and aristocratic principles which hold families at the top do

220

not operate as rigorously today; competitive forces emphasizing individual achievement function so that fewer sons of the elite stay at this high level than in the last generation. Competition is tougher not only for those fighting their way up to the top but for those fighting to stay there. Training to hold the high places against the vast armies of mobile men demands more time, more skill, as well as greater ability and fortitude. Many succumb; it will be remembered that a significantly larger percentage of the sons of the elite stayed in their fathers' positions in 1928 than do so now. Motivation today may be less for some; for many there seems to be an increased desire and willingness to make the hard preparation to hold to the level of their fathers.

These several developments probably mean that more men of ability, high skill, and professional training are getting into important jobs. If this be true, we can assume that more technical competence necessary for high performance is now being utilized and, since getting and keeping these jobs is based more on competition and less on birth, that those from both the lower and higher ranks must be better equipped to perform their tasks. Consistent with this is the fact that more men today spend longer periods of their lives in universities, colleges, and other professional schools training themselves for achievement. Since it is true that in the larger business enterprises there is more likelihood of men rising from lower levels, and since, compared with 1928, there appears to be an increasing number of the largest types of business and industry, it seems probable that the American economic world will continue to encourage competition and the rise of competent men.

The fluidity of the society and the freedom of choice of the individual in his fundamental life decisions can be measured also by the social and economic status of his mate. Since the descent of the child is determined by the position of his parents, occupation, marriage, and descent are closely interrelated and mutually influenced. Although a sizable percentage of the business elite married women of their own level, many married above or below. In other words, the basic caste rule of endogamy which fixes positions and rigidly closes ranks does not hold. Marriages outside the elite level also indicate there is considerable fluidity in present American society, that the upward movement of people is possible not only by occupational advancement but by marriage and, for the children of such marriages, by descent. Thus it is true to say that, while for some families, it is only two generations from shirtsleeves to shirtsleeves, for others it is but two or less from shirtsleeves to dinner jacket.

The incessant movement of many executives from place to place, state to state, region to region—all connected with their jobs and often with change from one position to another, and sometimes from one firm or industry to another—is an indication and expression of the circulation of the elite and also of the free movement of men in a fluid social and economic structure to which they are successfully relating themselves. Meanwhile they and their families must be flexible, learn and unlearn easily, fit themselves into many social and cultural situations which cluster around the job and life of the community. An executive in a great mail order house may advance for a few years in Chicago, transfer for promotion to the West Coast, then move down to Atlanta, and finally arrive back at a higher level in Chicago. His family, too, must continue readjusting themselves to each other, and actively participating in the schools, churches, and social life of the several communities, while the father and husband as a business leader manages his affairs so that each store and the great corporation of which it is a part are fitted profitably into the life of each city.

To survive, such people must know how to relate easily to others. They must have a realistic understanding of their world and possess a ready wit and ability to learn quickly about the people and the problems that confront them. Not only must they relate quickly and easily to others, but they must be able to detach themselves without too great emotional price. Although their interpersonal relations can be intimate and warm, these people cannot enjoy the assurance of permanent reinforcement of their emotional attachment by continued daily relations. Change, movement toward and away from things and people, involvement and disinvolvement, characterize many types of business careers and the lives of the families.

The consequences of this mode of life are important and numerous for our society. It means that we are developing a class of people at the upper reaches whose social world is not confined to the understandings, social assumptions, limitations, and world outlook of a single community or region. When the man from Atlanta moves to Chicago and the man from Boston goes to Atlanta and the two go on to Los Angeles and back to Chicago they and their families develop a sense of community that is beyond city or region or state. This sense of being in a national community and an integral part of a social world extending beyond one city is reinforced by the ceaseless movement of others, by daily travel, by the never-ending flow of messages and talk by telephone throughout the nation—and for some throughout the free world. Here all is change, all is activity, a part of the constant extension of an emergent society.

Meanwhile others, particularly those in the smaller industries who are more likely to be the sons of a birth elite, grow up and remain in the cities of their nativity. Their social and geographic positions remain fixed and their lives integrated with the life of their region and their cities. The center of their existence continues to be their home towns. The social and economic status groups to which they look for the meaning of who they are and what they do, and by which they are measured and controlled, are indigenous and local. The close relations which give meaning to existence are maintained through their lifetimes and, for many, through generations of fathers and sons. Intimacy, stability, measurement of self-achievement and social place, and understanding of the significance of events, of the self, and of others are defined by accumulated traditional usages and ordered meanings of the community. Birth to status and local community, growth of the self within them, and permanent location there produce a semi-closed society, a "fixed" group. Since a sizable percentage of the business men today are the sons of fathers of the business elite, the forces of rank are still powerful, particularly in the smaller enterprises in the smaller cities where family businesses continue to flourish.

The complex interrelations of the worlds of these "stable" people and those who circulate seem to be important and necessary parts of the moving equilibrium of the emergent American society. More people are on the move today; more acquire new kinds of jobs and move up and down than before. Since there is greater and greater choice of action, it is probable that there is more individual autonomy. This process is moderated and stabilized by the traditional factors of business and society, some of these centering around the strong life of the local community, others around the deep, powerful bonds of the family, and others around the many factors which combine to maintain a birth elite and the succession of fathers and sons to the same high positions.

There is no easy solution to the problem of maintaining the proper balance between the forces of movement and transition and the forces of persistence and inertia. The great division of labor made up of the important and the less important jobs which get the work done for the American collectivity is largely responsible for the continued advancement of our technology and economic enterprise, and the increased enrichment of our civilization. If this be true, the survival of our way of life in competition with other economic systems is greatly dependent on successfully filling these positions with competent, able men who have advanced and proved their ability in a freely competitive system.

The American credo that the best man should get the job is a sound one. This is the proper meaning of equality of opportunity. All qualified men and women of every social and racial background must be rewarded with promotions and pay to do the jobs necessary for the maintenance and advancement of this society and all its people. This must be true not only of powerful majorities dealing with members of minorities, but of powerful minorities dealing with members of the majority. Such is the proper secular meaning of the worth of the individual. He is valued and respected in his own right, but the respect and honor given him are expressions of his worth and his contribution to the collectivity. Occupational advancement and social achievement are the just rewards and expressions of competition, of successful functioning in jobs important to the firm and the industry and to the society and its people. There seems to be increasing evidence that most American business men recognize and are attempting to operate their businesses on these premises.

Advocacy of free competition, equality of opportunity, and getting the best qualified men for the job is easily said and agreed to, for each is an expression of values and principles basic to the traditional political and economic faith of most Americans. It is more difficult to say that these principles, like all others in the affairs of men as measured by the standards of a good society and the happiness of its people, can be carried too far.

Social pressure to take away *all* advantages from the sons of executives and administrators is not only revolutionary but dysfunctional in any society. Parents here, in Soviet Russia, and in all civilizations attempt to give their children the advantages of their own position. Societies such as ours, which emphasize the worth of the individual and equalitarian values, must use various methods to curb these parental urges of the rich, prestigeful, and powerful lest they succeed in creating a hereditary elite. This we have done and are progressively doing. To carry this to the point of eliminating all the sons of the elite from the arena of free competition, as some in their hostility wish to do, is as dangerous as it is absurd. Any elite will always help its children; the problem is to maintain a sensible balance between the hereditary forces of the family and those of achievement and individual opportunity and equality.

The number of men in the same firm as their fathers, compared with sons of the elite who achieve high position in other business organizations, is relatively small. There can be no doubt that each group of men was advantaged by being born to high estate. Only a few were directly aided by extra privileges and financial assistance;

but the immediate factor of being born to families accorded high rank by the community provides such fortunate men with social and economic advantages, such as being in the higher levels of prestige where the powerful are, going to the "right" preparatory schools, having the right social relations and clubs and fraternities in college, and going with and courting young women of their own social set, knowing what to do and not to do (while the parvenu by trial and error is struggling to learn that there are such ways). They get a head start in life that can be overcome only by hard work, grim determination, and watchfulness of personnel offices, or the eager quest of great corporations for young men of promise. The birth elite are advantaged because their families learn "superior" values, goals, and standards by living in the subculture of an upper class. Their earliest adaptations from infancy on— nursing, weaning, cleanliness, likes and dislikes, admiration or dislike of intimate figures about them, later childhood goals and ambitions—are set within the learning maze of a "superior" family.

To eliminate such advantages by any ordinary means, those short of revolution, is impossible. To destroy them entirely would necessitate a revolution to wipe out not only the top families but a family system which cares for its own. Violent revolutions led by frustrated men who hate all authority, including parental, have tried, but the family always reasserts itself. As long as society is orderly, and as long as the basic relations of the species, including mating, procreation, and caring for the young, are ordered and protected by the moral system, early advantages will be given to those born to high station.

The real problem of a free society that prizes equality and opportunity for all and competitive advantage for the able is to provide training situations, job opportunities, and methods for early identification of able youngsters from all economic levels who can be properly trained and prepared to move up to, and accept responsibility for, positions of power and prestige. If this generation has begun to solve the problem of free competition for prized jobs and there is more status fluidity and opportunity for all in

America today than previously, it is partly because we have developed a school system which reaches more children of the lower occupational levels. For them the school acts as a "foster parent," to help the ambitious learn the things the highly advantaged acquire in their home environments and social worlds.

There is more opportunity today, but there must be still more if the needs of business and of America are to be filled. Sons of laborers, because some of them had the opportunity to acquire the necessary superior learning, are at the top today who would not have been there yesterday. For the good of the society, many more should be. Although our present sample of big business men was drawn from the whole reservoir of American business leaders, at random, there were no Negroes among the men studied—eloquent testimony, if any were needed, that our country's selection of men of promise from the lower ranks sorts them in a biased manner. Only now are Negroes entering industrial management, reaching places at the bottom levels of the hierarchy as straw bosses where at least they become qualified as candidates for promotion. Although today Negroes are rapidly entering business and producing a solid and important middle class, thus strengthening their integration with, and loyalty to, America, it will take another generation for Negro men of ambition to climb the hard route now followed by some of the sons of the white middle class. Given the increasing recognition of the ability and social and personal worth of Negroes, it seems probable that they, too, will have their share of men in leadership. This achievement may be the ultimate test of free competition for jobs.

Although America's strides forward are energized and propelled by technological improvement and the successful use of the resources of a huge continent, it seems probable that the freeing of people by the "opening" of the social system to provide for individual autonomy and choice-making has allowed the streams of individual effort to pour into the great river of collective effort where the abilities, talents, and human energies of the masses carry us on to greater achievement. As long as we can keep the channels open and widen them, the energy of men will continue to surge into our collective life, keeping it vital and creative.

Education: Promotion, Pay, and Leadership in a Free Society

The principles of status advancement must operate in a free society to provide the rewards and supply the models, if striving men are to be sufficiently motivated to give their lives, their talents, and energies to the collectivity to use for its own advantage. To do this the system must be open to free competition. There are at least two kinds of competitors coming from the lower and middle levels to challenge the birth elite. They are the powerful, resolute men with little education who climb from job to job and, by enormous expenditures of energy—often with great talent and determination, and always with a feeling of inadequate training, reach the top, and the growing number of college trained men from the lower levels who compete with the first. Fewer and fewer of the "uneducated" achieve their ultimate goals; more often they remain as workers or in the lower levels of management.[1] Too many able men do not get an education and remain in the lower ranks, their talents lost or inadequately used by our society. The capacities of many of these men have never been fully tested. Although their intelligence is often high and their desire to succeed strong, they lack the broad education and sometimes the basic training to equip them for competition and to free them from a debilitating sense of inferiority which blocks their mobility. Often neither management nor they themselves recognize their own competence. More often modern management prefers to risk its money on college trained men. The increasing preference for college and professionaly trained men for managerial advancement has put a ceiling on the aspirations of a large majority of the workers, some

[1] W. Lloyd Warner and J. O. Low, *The Social System of the Modern Factory* (New Haven: Yale University Press, 1947); W. Lloyd Warner and Associates, *Democracy in Jonesville* (New York: Harper & Brothers, 1949); W. Lloyd Warner, *American Life: Dream and Reality* (Chicago: The University of Chicago Press, 1953).

of them able, because they are not so equipped. Often this arouses their hostility and resentment.

Management is doing serious damage to itself when it fails to promote from within and advances only those men who are college trained. Such a policy does get good men, but it creates bad labor relations while depriving itself of the services of its own staff. Policies for promotion must include both categories. If job aspirations and mobility to higher position are blocked because of educational deficiencies, programs can be (and in some firms are) instituted to remove them. There should be careful inventories of job specifications; there should be similar inventories of the worker's background and his social, personal, and technical skills. Training programs should also include encouragement to acquire skills in basic tool subjects, of reading, writing, arithmetic, and adequate English. Some of the successful men in our study confessed that they had been handicapped throughout their business careers because they had not learned the ordinary rudiments of arithmetic and standard English. Tens of thousands of workers are disadvantaged similarly to the point they cannot compete for advancement.

Adult education in America is a necessary process not only for equipping the mature with knowledge but for providing millions of Americans with more flexibility in their lives and greater freedom of choice, and so reducing the number of men and women confined to a fixed status. Correspondence schools, adult training programs of various kinds, night schools, as the present study indicates, are now helping perform this important service. Management should do its share. It should first clearly specify what educational skills are necessary for the various levels of advancement and then, not content, should provide counseling services to help the ambitious worker learn what he must do to equip himself. Most personnel offices have such knowledge about their employees; all educated and professionally trained men know where to acquire needed training. Relating job specifications and personnel assessment to knowledge about educational opportunities for adults is not difficult or expensive. A number of progressive companies are now using such a policy. Promotion from within must be not a pious, traditional precept of American business honored in word more than deed but an active program that encourages its own men to go ahead. Management should remember that many workers are aggressively hostile because they have lost hope for tomorrow.

Such a policy is not only just and sensible in using available human resources adequately but one of enlightened self-interest, not only for individual firms and industries but for the American economic order. All men, managers and workers, can feel they have a stake in the system, each can feel free, each can wish and hope for the future and share in the common vision. To most Americans occupational and social mobility are powerful incentive systems. When the channels are open to all and each man is free to compete if he will, it is unlikely that a technological and economic order that produces in such great abundance will be repudiated by those who enjoy its benefits.

But business and industry will increasingly rely on college and professionally trained men. A valuable study recently published by R. Clyde White, *These Will Go to College*,[2] demonstrates statistically not only that a large percentage of highly intelligent children from the lower occupational levels fail to go to college, but that all types of business and industry are demanding many more college trained men. More than three fourths of the industries studied were trying to hire more college trained men. Some industries, could they find them, would hire over a hundred per cent more college trained men than they now employ.

Given the educational needs of industry and society to train future leaders the question arises: What must we do to increase the number of men and women necessary to fill these important positions? Whose responsibility is it? How should this great task

[2] R. Clyde White, *These Will Go to College* (Cleveland: University of Western Reserve Press, 1952).

necessary for the advancement of our society be accomplished? What kinds of education are needed? Let us reassess the facts.

Business enterprises recruit their future managers from our institutions of higher learning. Colleges and professional schools no longer wait hopefully for the better students to come to them. They, too, actively recruit the able and the promising through scholarship and public relations programs, sometimes throughout the country. Recruitment of athletes may still be a competitive activity among the football universities, but more and more great universities of the highest quality are hunting for brilliant students. After a few years these scholars graduate and many of them once more are recruited, this time by industry. Whether recruited or not, thousands of them are the human resources on which the future success of modern American industry is founded. To survive, American business and our society must increase the proportions of our young people who are educated. Yet increasingly both private and public universities and colleges find difficulties in financing their present enterprises. High taxation has reduced the number of private donors. Public funds to support our state colleges and universities are being increased, but not sufficiently to meet the needs of the schools or of those they serve, including business, industry, government, and the professions.

If there is to be a solid foundation of learning on which business and industry can build and if there are to be professionally trained men and women to function satisfactorily in technical positions, industry and society must support education by taxation, and by the personal activities of owners and managers; industry itself must by endowment, fellowships, and other financial aids help support the professional schools and the liberal arts colleges. It takes little imagination and only practical sense to know that it is wise to support such schools as Harvard's Graduate School of Business Administration or the California Institute of Technology. What they teach is functional and necessary for business administration and the operation of great industrial technologies such as Du Pont. Good as such education is and wise and generous as such support may be, they are not enough. Those business leaders who speak and act on the principle that "what's good for America is good for us and American enterprise" are more nearly correct. If business men and business enterprises are risk takers, they risk their businesses and personal futures as parts of the great American adventure where free men can choose their course of action, their collective wisdom and freedom to choose ultimately determining whether our civilization will survive or be destroyed. American business itself must have well trained leaders, but above all, American business and all America need great leaders for the collective risk-taking of a free society. The fact that a large proportion of our present business leaders receive their college training at liberal arts colleges is eloquent testimony to the importance of such institutions in training American leaders.

Technological schools are important and necessary parts of our scientific system, but they, too, are dependent on the liberal arts to prepare their students and enrich their lives. The business leader of today is something more than a technological expert; he is a manager of men, and increasingly he is also playing what he and business enterprise know to be his proper role as a citizen in the larger cultural and social life of the community. He must be an economic agent and an administrator and also a citizen who understands and acts on the principles and values of a civilization founded on the precepts that each individual is valuable not only for the work he does and for his contribution to our common enterprises but, above all, for what he is as a human being. Perhaps no part of our changing society is more dedicated to the maintenance and creative transmission of these intellectual, cultural, and spiritual principles than our institutions of higher learning. Located throughout the country, they function like great cultural reservoirs collecting and containing the significant life streams of yesterday and today to supply and refresh the collective life with their creative energies. They can remain strong and grow in their life-giving power only as long as the individuals and the institutions which depend upon them and benefit from them sustain and support them.

The great industries which produce in such abundance must learn how to help the colleges and universities solve their economic problems and continue autonomous and free to maintain traditional learning and wisdom as well as develop the physical, biological, and social sciences. Thus they will serve the society by allowing the older generation to transmit the best of its heritage to the young, who can receive it and recreate it, transforming the traditional values, beliefs, and practices of the past into the new adaptive ones of today and tomorrow.

Each society, ours particularly, has its semi-sacred beliefs of what man is and what he should be. They are the living values and concepts of the collectivity about what it is, what its people want and do not want, and what they should and should not be. As such, a society's "myths" are never false. They act as witnesses especially for the spiritual and biological nature of man, for in them man speaks for himself, and through them he often believes that God, too, speaks for Himself and for man. During its long history our society has been blessed with a number of significant sacred and secular myths about the nature of human existence, of which two, in a multitude of forms, have cried out the meaning of man and his ultimate fate. In one, man (the hero and leading character) must learn to resign himself to the powerful external forces which decide his fate. His task is to subordinate his own needs for today and his individual hopes for tomorrow to a spiritual or secular force, perhaps to a materialistic one of economic change or revolution, or to spiritual demands of a sacred being. The hero learns through resignation of his self and his life to a superior external force or being.

The other basic belief-system is a myth of human triumph. In it the hero struggles and overcomes external obstacles; he encounters and ultimately triumphs over the persons and forces of evil; he may confess his doubt and his desire to admit defeat, but he never resigns himself to whatever may happen to him. Yesterday this hero was a knight fighting his way forward to ultimate victory, or an ascetic who conquered the evil beings who waylaid him as he pressed onward to seek and find good. Today the hero may be the scientist who seeks and finds the solution to a problem for the benefit of man or a poor boy who, through pluck, skill, and a good heart, works his way to the top. The latter often is the business man who, starting at the bottom, solves the vexing problems of business enterprise and climbs upward to triumph over all obstacles. Each myth has its simple version that even children can understand. Horatio Alger, often mentioned by the business leaders as an important influence in their lives, embodies this myth of man's triumph and his progress from rags to riches. The success stories lived by these business leaders also express and evoke the myth of human triumph. In them men triumph over fate; in them a changing, hopeful society, believing in tomorrow and energetically struggling today to make tomorrow true, finds some of the vital strength necessary to drive onward toward the attainment of tomorrow's goals.

Acknowledgments

The authors are indebted to a large number of people for their generous assistance in helping us with the research and preparation of the book. We first wish to express our gratitude to the business leaders themselves; without their collaboration the study would have been impossible. Several prominent business men publicly sponsored our research and vouched for us to the world of business. For their special service and their wise and helpful counsel we wish to thank:

Lawrence A. Appley of New York City
John Cowles of Minneapolis
Clarence B. Randall of Chicago
Frank Stanton of New York City
General Robert E. Wood of Chicago

Another group of leaders advised us on problems having to do with relating our research to business enterprise. Their guidance was much appreciated. Among these men were:

W. G. Caples of Chicago
L. H. Fisher of St. Paul
Howard Goodman of Chicago
James C. Worthy of Chicago

While we were designing our research and attempting to solve many perplexing scientific problems we were helped by the skill and knowledge provided by our academic colleagues. We wish to thank Professor Phillip Hauser, Theodore Shultz, and William E. Henry of the University of Chicago, and Dr. Burleigh B.

235

Gardner and Harriette Moore of Social Research Inc. of Chicago. Our able and highly skilled research staff supplied us with invaluable research evidence. For this we must thank Sarah Wheeler, Ira Glick, Robert W. Schofield, and Alice Chandler. Thanks should be given to the National Opinion Research Center for their help with the statistical part of the research. We wish to thank Mildred Hall Warner for her invaluable editorial assistance.

Several middlewestern business men and business enterprises contributed substantially to our financial support. We wish to thank:

E. B. Busby of R. Donnelley & Sons Company, Chicago
Goodman Manufacturing Company, Chicago
Inland Steel Company, Chicago
Sears, Roebuck & Company, Chicago
Marshall Field, Chicago and New York

Although their aid was most generous, our largest contributor was The Louis W. and Maud Hill Foundation. They not only supported the first half of our study but paid for all of the second part.

Our gratitude must be expressed to three men in particular for their individual support and encouragement. Howard Goodman's and James Worthy's early interest in the problem of social mobility in business enterprise encouraged us to start the study and carry it through to completion. A. A. Heckman's understanding of the scientific and practical significance of the study and his many valuable suggestions were sources of real strength throughout the research.

Finally we wish to thank our own university for its backing. This was not the passive support of a great institution of learning but the active aid of interested men. Chancellor Lawrence Kimpton and George H. Watkins were particularly active on our behalf.

Although we have expressed our respect, not to say our admiration, for the earlier research by Professors Taussig and Joslyn we must not let this opportunity pass to thank them for their splendid study.

Methodological Note

It is impossible to provide a full statement here on the methods and techniques used to study business leaders. The whole of Chapter VIII in *Occupational Mobility in American Business and Industry, 1928–1952*, by W. Lloyd Warner and James Abegglen (The University of Minnesota Press, 1955) is devoted to this task. This same technical volume also supplies many additional tables on the details of the research.

In general the research went through two phases: in the first we solicited statistical information about the careers of business men from leaders throughout the United States; in the second, we obtained detailed interviews and psychological studies of representative leaders and their wives. The four-page schedule, sent to 17,546 leaders and returned by 8562 of them, contained the questions which supplied the quantitative evidence for this volume. Complete anonymity was guaranteed and maintained. Only the authors knew the names of the respondents; their schedules were identified by numbers. The evidence was given the usual tests and passed them for representativeness, reliability, validity, and in general trustworthiness for telling the truth about the lives of business men. The reader will see that the research was designed to make it possible to compare our results, step by step, with those of the 1928 study, and thus tell us something about trends and the direction in which business enterprise is moving.

The intensive studies were detailed interviews of some two hours or more which usually took place in each man's office and at his home. The business leader was interviewed at each place to give us knowledge about how he appeared in these two principal centers of his existence. The wife was interviewed in the home. The interviews with the women told us much about their husbands.

The evidence about the personalities of the leader and his wife came from the interviews and from the Thematic Apperception Test. Social science was first indebted to Professor Henry Murray of Harvard University for the TAT and then to Professor William Henry for significant modifications to make it more useful in social studies. As is well known the test is a series of vaguely structured pictures. The respondent is asked to tell a story about each; through the words he utters in so doing he projects his own psychic life on the several pictures. From them the skilled analyst, particularly when aided by depth interviewing, can learn much about the respondent's personality and the way he fits himself into his social world.

The information about the psychic life of the leader and his wife told us about how each contributed to his "success story," and what part the personality factor played. These human documents answered many of the questions raised by our statistical results and turned their cold significances into the warm life of human beings with their frustrations and defeats and their achievements and victories. From them we learned the "inside" story of success.

Index

239